职教名校
申请手册

通职中文联盟 主编

清华大学出版社
北京

内 容 简 介

本书为满足各国学生留学中国学习职业技能的需求而编写，参照中国特色高水平高职学校和专业建设计划（以下简称"双高计划"），结合各省市重点职业院校名录，遴选出了一些职业院校，并从学校简介、历史沿革、专业设置及奖学金情况、学校行政管理制度及职教高考情况和校园文化等多方面对这些职业学校进行介绍。为了便于学生尽快筛选出符合自己条件的学校，书中也将每个学校的申请条件等单独附录列出。

本书为有意来中国就读的国际学生及其家长提供一个相对系统和全面的信息与资料，也可以作为国内读者了解中国职业院校的参考资料。

本书封面贴有清华大学出版社防伪标签，无标签者不得销售。
版权所有，侵权必究。举报：010-62782989，beiqinquan@tup.tsinghua.edu.cn。

图书在版编目（CIP）数据

职教名校申请手册 / 通职中文联盟主编 .—北京：清华大学出版社，2023.10
ISBN 978-7-302-64883-3

Ⅰ.①职… Ⅱ.①通… Ⅲ.①中等专业学校–申请–手册 Ⅳ.① G718.3

中国国家版本馆 CIP 数据核字（2023）第 200087 号

责任编辑：陈　明　李益倩
封面设计：常雪影
责任校对：赵琳爽
责任印制：曹婉颖

出版发行：清华大学出版社
网　　址：https://www.tup.com.cn, https://www.wqxuetang.com
地　　址：北京清华大学学研大厦A座　　邮　编：100084
社 总 机：010-83470000　　邮　购：010-62786544
投稿与读者服务：010-62776969, c-service@tup.tsinghua.edu.cn
质量反馈：010-62772015, zhiliang@tup.tsinghua.edu.cn

印 装 者：小森印刷（北京）有限公司
经　　销：全国新华书店
开　　本：185mm×260mm　　印　张：5.75　　字　数：91千字
版　　次：2023 年 10 月第 1 版　　印　次：2023 年 10 月第 1 次印刷
定　　价：49.00 元

产品编号：096459-01

编 委 会

主　　编：王锦红

副 主 编：钟国兴

编　　委：何朝晖　范俊杰　曹静　程利生　张雯君　陈世超
　　　　　华磊　刘沛然　刘璐

前言

职业教育的发展体现一个国家的经济发展水平和教育现代化水平。在中国,职业教育包括中职、高职专科、高职本科及以上办学层次,涵盖了从基础教育到高等教育的各个层次。目前,中国通过推动"职教高考"等方式建立现代职业教育体系,完善学历上升通道和纵向贯通。从上升通道看,当前职业教育中外合作项目已经实现了学历贯通,助推学生的学历上升实现可持续发展。

联合国教科文组织把职业教育称为技术与职业教育和培训(technical and vocational education and training, TVET)。这一点在中国的职业院校中践行得比较好。中国的职业院校从发起到发展升级,都需要与就业市场和企业紧密结合。它独有的产教融合、校企合作的优势,强化工学结合、实训、模块化的教育教学活动,将中国特色的学徒制作为主要的培养形式,使学生毕业即可上手,就业单位满意度和毕业生工作稳定程度大幅度提高。

中国的职业院校在国家的大力推动下,紧跟社会人才需求,积极调整专业设置和人才培养模式,使毕业生更好地与就业市场衔接。职业院校的新增专业也紧贴企业需求,将培育计划与企业人才计划紧密结合。全国职业院校已开设 1300 余个专业和 10 余万个专业点。2021 年,教育部发布的新版《职业教育专业简介》中统计中等职业教育新增 28 个专业,高职专科新增 74 个专业,高职本科新增 167 个专业。

对于职业院校的选择与综合类大学不同,要更加关注产业方向,不同职业院校的专业设置、就业市场与其地方产业基础、已有架构、合作企业有较大的关联,本书的目的是为学生和家长在择校时提供一份"一本通"的手册。书中包括知名职业院校的介绍、专业设置、往年就业市场数据等内容,便于学生和家长做出最优选择。

在职业院校的选择方面,我们主要参照国家"双高计划"及地方重点职业院校名录。有些职业院校正在努力提升自己的办学质量,准备参与国家"双高计划"评选,本书仅包括图书出版之前的职业院校名录。本书将从以下几个方面对职业院校做介绍。

1. 学校简介：这一部分主要介绍学校的所在地、性质、基础设施、"双高"建设情况，目前的规模（在校学生人数、生师比）、近年来学生总体就业率等。

2. 历史沿革：主要介绍学校的专业发展历程、教育方针和特色，发现其经典专业和新设专业，以便把握其培养周期和就业比例的关系。

3. 专业设置及奖学金情况：专业设置是了解和选择职业院校的重点参考内容，一般来说，开设已久的传统专业就业数据比较稳定，新兴专业就业市场缺口比较大。书中将列出近年来专业就业数据、就业重点分布企业类型、企业定向培养的专业数据发现。其中涵盖新兴专业如"智能化、数字化"的职业院校，书中将重点介绍其师资配置、联合培养企业等。另外还会介绍学校往年的奖学金数额、申请条件和申请成功比例。

4. 学校行政管理制度及职教高考情况：学校的管理制度反映其办学宗旨、理念、传统，有助于学生了解自身目标、理念和学校的匹配度。对于有专升本培养的职业院校，书中会介绍专升本培养步骤，便于有继续学历提升要求的学生做出选择。

5. 校园文化：职业院校与大学一样，学生都将在学校学习、生活数年时间，校园文化对个人的校园生活会产生众多影响。这部分将重点介绍学校的校园社团文化建设、文化体育活动、特殊节庆日、社会公共活动、与兄弟院校的互动情况等。

为了方便读者快速获取信息，本书将涉及入学考试、入学条件等内容附在正文之后。在有限的篇幅内，本书只对各职业院校作基本的介绍，不作评价和排名，若有疏漏和差错，希望读者多谅解并给予指正。

编者
2023年3月

Preface

The development of vocational education mirrors a country's level of economic development and modernization of education. China's vocational education includes secondary level, junior college level, undergraduate level and above, covering all levels of education from basic education to higher education. Currently, China is establishing a modern vocational education system by promoting methods such as the "Vocational Education College Entrance Examination", facilitating the access to upward channels and vertical pass-through for students to improve their academic qualifications. From the perspective of upward channels, the current Sino-foreign cooperation projects in vocational education have achieved education continuity, helping students obtain higher education degrees in a sustainable way.

The United Nations Educational, Scientific and Cultural Organization (UNESCO) refers to vocational education as technical and vocational education and training (TVET) and China's vocational colleges has achieved effective implementation in this aspect. From the stage of initiation to upgrading, China's vocational colleges need to closely combine with the job market and the relative enterprises. They have unique advantages of integrating industry and education, school-enterprise cooperation, carry out the teaching activities of emphasizing the combination of theory and practice, practical training, and modularized learning, and take the traditional apprenticeship system as the main training form, so that students can start their job immediately after graduation, having greatly improved the satisfaction of employers and the job stability of graduates.

Under the vigorous push from the government, China's vocational colleges have actively adjusted their majors and talent training models in response to the needs of the social talent market demand, enabling graduates to better adapt to the job market. The newly added majors of vocational colleges also closely cater to the needs of enterprises, combing the college's training program closely with enterprise's talent program. There are now more than 1,300 majors and over 100,000 major construction sites offered in vocational colleges nationwide. In 2021, the newly-revised *Introduction to Vocational Education Majors* Ministry of Education includes 28 newly-added majors in secondary vocational education, 74 newly-added majors at the junior college level, and 167 newly-added majors at the undergraduate level.

Different from choosing comprehensive universities, the choice of vocational colleges requires more attention to industry orientation. The major settings and its job market of different vocational colleges are closely related to their local industrial foundation, existing structure, and cooperative enterprises. This book aims to offer a "one-stop" guide for students and their parents when choosing a vocational college. In this book, 18 leading vocational institutions' profiles, major settings, and employment market data from previous years will make it easier for students and their parents to make the best choice.

In the selection of vocational colleges, we mainly refer to the national "Double High-Level Plan" and the list of key vocational colleges in the local area. Some vocational colleges are striving to improve their education quality and are preparing to participate in the selection of the national "Double High-Level

Plan". This book only includes the list of vocational colleges before its publication. The book will introduce vocational colleges from the following aspects.

1. School profile: This section mainly introduces the college from its location, nature, infrastructure, "Double High-Level Plan" construction, current size (number of students in school, student-to-teacher ratio), and overall employment rate of students in recent years, etc.

2. History: This section mainly introduces the college's professional development process, educational policies and characteristics, and displays its classic majors and newly-established majors in order to grasp the relationship between its training cycle and employment ratio.

3. Major setting and scholarship situation: Major setting is the key indicator for understanding and choosing a vocational college. Generally speaking, the employment data of long-established traditional majors is relatively easily accessible, however, the emerging majors have a large gap in their employmentmarket data. The book will list the employment data of different majors in recent years, the enterprise types with key employment distribution, and the data of majors of oriented training for enterprises.It also includes the emerging majors in some vocational colleges such as intelligentization and digitization, with a focus on their teacher allocation and joint training enterprises, etc. In addition, the book will introduce their scholarship amounts in previous years, application requirements and the application percentage of successful applications.

4. School administrative management system and the situation of Vocational Education College Entrance Examination: The management system of a college reflects its educational mission, ideas and tradition, which helps students estimate the matching degree between their own goals, ideas and that of the college. For vocational colleges with upgrading programs for bachelor's degree, the book will introduce the training steps to facilitate the students with a need of further education.

5. Campus culture: Like comprehensive universities, the students in vocational colleges will spend several years studying and living on campus, and the campus culture will have many influences on their personal life. This section will focus on the vocational colleges' campus cultural construction of clubs, cultural and sports activities, special festivals, social public activities, and interaction with their peer colleges.

To facilitate the readers' quick access to the relative information, this book places the content related to the entrance exams and admission requirements in the appendixes. Due to its limited space, this book only provides basic introductions to each vocational colleges, without evaluations and rankings. If there are omissions or errors, we hope that the tolerant readers will point them out to us.

Editor
March, 2023

目录

深圳职业技术大学	1
重庆电子工程职业学院	6
重庆公共运输职业学院	11
浙江机电职业技术学院	15
南京信息职业技术学院	19
陕西能源职业技术学院	23
北京经济管理职业学院	27
重庆工程职业技术学院	34
潍坊职业学院	37
北京工业职业技术学院	41
西安翻译学院	44
陕西国防工业职业技术学院	47
重庆工商大学派斯学院	50
重庆人文科技学院	52
湖北职业技术学院	55
重庆城市管理职业学院	58
重庆应用技术职业学院	62
云南大学滇池学院	65
日历	68

CONTENTS

Shenzhen Polytechnic University —————————————————————————— 1

Chongqing College of Electronic Engineering ———————————————— 6

Chongqing Vocational College of Public Transportation ————————— 11

Zhejiang Institute of Mechanical & Electrical Engineering ———————— 15

Nanjing Vocational College of Information Technology ————————— 19

Shaanxi Energy Institute ——————————————————————————— 23

Beijing Institute of Economics and Management —————————————— 27

Chongqing Vocational Institute of Engineering —————————————— 34

Weifang Vocational College ————————————————————————— 37

Beijing Polytechnic College ————————————————————————— 41

Xi'an Fanyi University ——————————————————————————— 44

Shaanxi Institute of Technology ——————————————————————— 47

Pass College of Chongqing Technology & Business University ————— 50

Chongqing College of Humanities, Science & Technology ——————— 52

Hubei Polytechnic Institute ————————————————————————— 55

Chongqing City Management College ———————————————————— 58

Chongqing Vocational College of Applied Technology ————————— 62

Dianchi College of Yunnan University ——————————————————— 65

Calendar ——————————————————————————————————— 68

学校介绍 School Profile

深圳职业技术大学
Shenzhen Polytechnic University

院校风采 Institutional Charm | 许建领 XU Jianling

深圳职业技术大学校长许建领
XU Jianling, President of Shenzhen Polytechnic University

许建领

　　光阴如梭，岁月流金。1993年建校以来，深圳职业技术大学始终秉承特区"敢为天下先"的改革创新精神，锐意进取，一路开拓，从首届59名学生到如今30 000余名在校生，从最初的借用校舍到拥有环境优美、设施优良的六大校区，从默默无闻到广受关注、蜚声海外的一流高职院校，学校成功地走出了一条中国特色高等职业教育发展之路，创造了中国高职教育的多个第一，综合实力稳居全国同类院校前列，连续多年位居全国高职高专院校竞争力排行榜首位。

The years fly by but the glorious history continues. Since the establishment of Shenzhen Polytechnic University (SZPT) in 1993, with adherence to the reform and innovation spirit of "daring to be the first in the world" in the Shenzhen Special Economic Zone, it has always been forging ahead and a pathfinder in vocational education. From the first batch of 59 students to over 30,000 students today, from the initial borrowed school buildings to the six campuses with beautiful environment and excellent facilities, from obscurity to a noticeable and well-known first-class vocational college at home and abroad, SZPT has successfully stepped out of a road of higher vocational education development with Chinese characteristics, and keep the first position in many areas in China's higher vocational education. And its comprehensive strength has remained at the forefront of similar colleges in China, and it has consistently ranked first in the national competitiveness ranking of vocational colleges for many years.

立志如山，行道如水。在新的历史节点上，深圳职业技术大学将继续充分利用区域与自身优势，努力成为职业教育创新发展的先行者、复合式创新型高素质技术技能人才的摇篮、企业家的摇篮、深圳中小微企业技术研发中心、深圳市民终身教育学校与中国职业教育师资培训的重要基地，率先建成中国特色、世界一流的职业院校，为世界职业教育发展贡献"深圳模式"。

With lofty aspirations and pragmatic wisdom, at the new historical juncture, Shenzhen Polytechnic University will continue to make full use of its regional and institutional advantages to become a pioneer in vocational education innovation and development, a cradle for compound innovative high-quality technical and skilled talents, a cradle for entrepreneurs, a technology research and development center for small and medium-sized enterprises in Shenzhen, a lifelong education school for the citizens of Shenzhen, and an important base for teacher training in China's vocational education. SZPT will take the lead in building a world-class vocational college with Chinese characteristics, setting the "Shenzhen Model" for the development of vocational education in the world.

院校风采 Institutional Charm | 王隆杰 WANG Longjie

深圳职业技术大学王隆杰教授
WANG Longjie, Professor of Shenzhen Polytechnic University

广东省教学名师，获得中国国家教学成果特等奖。有八年的软件开发和网络管理经历，以及二十年职业教育经历，目前从事网络(Network)技术、云计算(Cloud Computing)技术、网络安全(Cyber Security)技术的教学。2005年通过思科路由交换(Router&Switch)CCIE认证、2008年通过思科安全(Security)学。2018年通过华为云计算(Cloud)HCIE认证，还通过了微软(Microsoft)、亚亚马逊(AWS)、红帽(Redhat)等二十个IT认证。把领先的ICT技术和认证引入到职业教育，促进了学生技能的提升，220名学生通过思科CCIE认证，80名学生通过华为HCIE

王隆杰

认证。编写《思科CCNA实验指南》《网络攻防案例教程》等十余本教材，多次指导学生获得思科网络技术大赛、华为ICT技能大赛、中国职业院校技能大赛的奖项。制作了十多门网络课程，学习人数达845万人次。

WANG Longjie is a famous teacher in Guangdong Province who was awarded the Special Prize for National Teaching Achievements in China. He has 8 years of experience in software development and network management, and 20 years of vocational education experience. He is currently engaged in teaching Network Technology, Cloud Computing Technology and Cyber Security Technology. In 2005, he passed the Cisco Router & Switch CCIE certification. In 2008, he passed the Cisco Security CCIE certification, and in 2018, he passed the Huawei Cloud Computing HCIE certification. He also received 20 IT certifications such as Microsoft, Amazon Web Services (AWS), and Redhat. He introduced the leading ICT technologies and certifications into vocational education, improving students' skills, with 220 students receiving Cisco CCIE certification and 80 students receiving Huawei HCIE certification. He has compiled more than 10 textbooks such as *Cisco CCNA Experiment Guide and Network Attack and Defense Case Tutorial*. Under his guidance, his students won awardssuch as Cisco Network Technology Competition, Huawei ICT Skills Competition and China Vocational College Skills Competition for many times. He has produced more than 10 online courses, with a total of 8.45 million learners.

历史 History

深圳职业技术大学创建于1993年，是国内最早独立举办高等职业技术教育的院校之一。建校以来，深圳职业技术学校艰苦创业，开拓进取，不断创新教育教学理念、办学体制机制和人才培养模式，创造了中国高职教育的多个第一。学校依托珠三角产业发展，秉承深圳特区改革创新精神，坚持把立德树人作为学校教育的根本任务，立足于职业教育产教融合的办学特色，各项事业取得骄人成绩，被誉为中国高职教育的领军学校。学校始终坚持为国家服务、为深圳社会经济服务、为学生健康成长成才服务，致力于建设高层次技术技能人才培养高地、产教融合高地，努力创建中国特色、世界一流的职业院校，为推动中国职业教育创新发展做出积极贡献。

Founded in 1993, Shenzhen Polytechnic University is one of the earliest institutions in China to independently offer higher vocational and technical education. Since its establishment, SZPT has been forging ahead with painstaking efforts, constantly innovating the teaching philosophy, school-running system and talent training models, thereby maintaining the first position in many areas in China's higher vocational education. Relying on the industrial development in the Pearl River Delta region, SZPT adheres to the spirit of reform and innovation of the Shenzhen Special Economic Zone, and takes moral education as the fundamental task of the college. Based on the characteristics of integrating production and education in vocational education, SZPT has made remarkable achievements in various undertakings, and is known as a leading college in China's higher vocational education. SZPT has always been insisting on serving the country, Shenzhen's socio-economic development, and the healthy growth and success of students. It is committed to building a highland for cultivating high-level technical and skilled talents, as well as a highland for integrating industry and education. It strives to create a world-class vocational college with Chinese characteristics, and actively contributes to promoting the innovative development of vocational education in China.

成就 Achievements

建校以来，学校扎根深圳，与特区共成长，取得了优异的办学成绩。2001年成为首家通过国家示范性高职院校实践教学基地优秀评估的院校，2009年通过国家示范性高等职业院校建设项目验收，成为我国高等职业教育领域首批国家级示范校。2019年成功入选中国特色高水平高职学校和专业建设计划A档建设单位。2021年7月，深圳职业技术大学探索构建的"六融合""六个共同"产教深度融合模式被国家发展改革委列入向全国推广借鉴的"深圳经验"。

Since its establishment, SZPT has been rooted in Shenzhen, grown together with the Shenzhen Special Economic Zone, achieving excellent academic performance. In 2001, it became the first institution to pass the quality evaluation of practice teaching base of national model higher vocational colleges. In 2009, it passed the acceptance of the national model higher vocational college construction project and became one of the first batch of national model higher vocational colleges. In 2019, it was successfully selected as the A-level construction unit of high-level vocational colleges and majors with Chinese characteristics. In July 2021, the "Six Integrations" and "Six Commons" models of deep integration of industry and education explored by SZPT was listed by the National Development and Reform Commission as one of the "Shenzhen Experiences" to be promoted nationwide.

专业 Major

学校现有专业88个，所有专业对接深圳主导产业、支柱产业和战略性新兴产业及优势产业；建立14个专业群，每个专业群含3个以上专业，随产业动态调整机制，专业(群)结构合理。现所有专业均招收外国留学生，比如计算机网络技术、学前教育、软件技术、现代物流管理、金融服务与管理、智能制造工程技术、现代通信工程、电子信息工程技术、数字动画等专业。

SZPT currently has 88 majors, all of which are connected with Shenzhen's leading industries, pillar industries, strategic emerging industries and advantageous industries. It has established 14 major clusters, each of which contains more than 3 majors, with a timely adjustment in accordance with the industries dynamics to keep a reasonable structure of majors (cluster). All majors now admit foreign students, such as Computer Network Technology, Preschool Education, Software Technology, Modern Logistics Management, Financial Services and Management, Intelligent Manufacturing Engineering Technology, Modern Communication Engineering, Electronic Information Engineering Technology, Digital Animation, etc.

建校时间 Founding time	1993年	专业 Majors	88个
教师人数 Number of teachers	1441	开学时间 Commencement time	秋季9月、春季3月
学生人数 Number of students	24 257	学习年限 Years of study	1~2年预科或者3年全日制学历留学生

报名联络 Registration Contact

通信地址：广东省深圳市南山区留仙大道7098号

邮编：518055

联系电话：86-0755-26731132

联系人：邹老师

电子邮箱：ieszpt@szpt.edu.cn； zougeng@szpt.edu.cn

Address: No. 7098, Liuxian Avenue, Nanshan District, Shenzhen, Guangdong, China
Postcode: 518055
Tel: 86-0755-26731132
Contact: Mr. Zou
Email: ieszpt@szpt.edu.cn; zougeng@szpt.edu.cn

学校介绍 School Profile

重庆电子工程职业学院
Chongqing College of Electronic Engineering

院校风采 Institutional Charm | 孙卫平 SUN Weiping

重庆电子工程职业学院孙卫平教授
SUN Weiping, Professor of Chongqing College of Electronic Engineering

孙卫平

　　二级教授，国务院特殊津贴专家。主要从事教育教学管理工作的研究，先后在《光明日报》《中国职业技术教育》《职业教育研究》《中国成人教育》《职教论坛》《中国高等教育》等重要核心期刊发表论文10余篇，主持和主研了"高职毕业生就业问题与对策研究"等省部级高职教育研究课题10余项，主持编写专著1部，其中主持完成的教学成果《面向西部，实施全程工学结合的电子信息类专业"四环相扣"教学模式改革》荣获第六届高等教育国家级教学成果一等奖，《匠师协同·双能支撑·孵扶联动：电子信息类专业能工巧匠培养模式创新与实践》获得重庆市教学成果特等奖。曾获"新中国成立60周年重庆教育功勋人物""重庆市优秀专业技术人才""第六届黄炎培职业教育奖杰出校长奖"等多项荣誉。

Second-Tier Professor, Expert enjoying special allowance of the State Council. He is mainly engaged in the research of education and teaching management, and has published more than 10 papers in important core journals such as *Guangming Daily, China Vocational and Technical Education, Vocational Education Research, China Adult Education, Vocational Education Forum,* and *China Higher Education.* He has presided over and conducted more than 10 higher vocational education research projects at provincial and ministerial level, such as Research on Employment Problems and Countermeasures of Higher vocational Graduates, and presided over the compilation of one monograph. Several teaching results under his supervision have won different awards, among which *Facing the West, Implementing the Reform of the "Four-Loop Interconnection" Teaching Model* for Electronic Information Majors with a Whole Process of Combining Work and Learning won the First Prize of the Sixth National Teaching Achievement of Higher Education, and *Collaboration of Artisan and Teacher · Dual-Energy Support · Incubation and Support Interaction: The Innovation and Practice of Cultivating Skilled Craftsmen in Electronic Information Majors* won the Special Prize of Chongqing Municipal Teaching Achievement. He has won many honors such as Chongqing Education Meritorious Person for the 60th Anniversary of the Founding of New China, Chongqing Excellent Professional and Technical Talents, Outstanding President Award of the 6th Huang Yanpei Vocational Education Award, and so on.

院校风采 聂强
Institutional Charm NIE Qiang

重庆电子工程职业学院院长聂强
NIE Qiang, President of Chongqing College of Electronic Engineering

博士、教授、重庆英才创新创业领军人才、巴渝学者特聘教授、西南大学博士生导师、享受国务院政府特殊津贴专家；重庆电子工程职业学院院长；中国高等教育学会理事、中国高等教育学会职业技术教育分会副理事长、重庆高等教育学会副会长、中国职业技术教育学会学术委员会委员；中国高等教育学会高校竞赛评估与管理体系研究专家委员会委员、教育部职业院校质量发展研究中心质量评估专业委员会主任委员。在《光明日报》《学术界》《中国职业技术教育》等重要核心期刊发表论文40余篇，主编高等职业教育重点建设规划教材、精品课示范性规划教材等7部。主持国家级职业教育专业教学资源库1项，主持教育部专项课题、重庆市教育科学规划重大项目、教学改革重大项目等国家级、省级及以上课题10余项。作为第一完成人，先后获国家级教学成果二等

聂 强

奖、重庆市教学成果特等奖和重等奖和重庆第六届优秀教育科研成果二等奖等荣誉。

Doctor, professor, Chongqing's leading talent in innovation and entrepreneurship, Distinguished Professor of Bayu Scholars, Doctoral Supervisor of Southwest University, Expert enjoying special allowance of the State Council, President of Chongqing College of Electronic Engineering, Director of China Association of Higher Education, Vice Chairman of Vocational and Technical Education Branch of China Association of Higher Education, Vice president of Chongqing Association of Higher Education, Member of Academic Committee of China Association of Vocational and Technical Education, Member of Expert Committee of Research on Competition Evaluation and Management System of Colleges and Universities of China Higher Education Society, and Chairman of Professional Committee of Quality Evaluation of Vocational College Quality Development Research Center under the Ministry of Education. He has published more than 40 papers in important core journals such as *Guangming Daily Academics* and *China Vocational and Technical Education*, and edited 7 textbooks including key construction planning textbooks and exemplary planning textbooks of high-quality courses for higher vocational education. He has presided over one national teaching resource library for vocational education and more than 10 national and provincial level projects such as special projects under the Ministry of Education, major projects of Chongqing education science planning and major projects of teaching reform. As the leading author, he has won the Second Prize of National Teaching Achievements, the Special Prize of Chongqing Teaching Achievements, and the Second Prize of the 6th Excellent Education and Research Achievements of Chongqing.

历史 History

重庆电子工程职业学院始建于1965年，位于重庆大学城，地处西部(重庆)科学城"智核区"，是重庆市政府举办、重庆市教委主管的全日制普通高等院校，是国家在西部地区重点建设的中国特色高水平高职学校。在长期的办学历程中，学校坚持"人才强校、文化兴校、特色立校"的发展理念，秉承"厚德强能、求实创新"的校训，传承"龙翔马跃、博润致远"的人文精神，形成"智联六合、信安九州"的办学特色，主动服务国家发展、服务区域经济社会发展。

Chongqing College of Electronic Engineering, founded in 1965, is located in the "intellectual core area" of the Western (Chongqing) Science City. It is a full-time general higher education institution sponsored by Chongqing Municipal Government and supervised by Chongqing Municipal Education Commission and is a high-level vocational institution with Chinese characteristics in the western region which the country gives priority to. During its long history of operation, it adheres to the development philosophy of "strong talents, prosperous culture and unique characteristics", and abides by the institution motto of "with great virtue and outstanding capacity, seeking truth and innovation", and inherits the humanistic spirit of "aiming high, reaching far", forms the school-running philosophy of "intelligent coalition with the forces from all sides and constant faithfulness to gain credibility", and actively serves national development and regional economic and social development.

成就 Achievements

重庆电子工程职业学院坚持国际化办学,是高等职业院校"世界竞争力50强",中非(重庆)职业教育联盟中方理事长单位,全国唯一获批第46届世界技能大赛中国集训主、辅基地并拥有2名中国专家组组长的高职院校。教育部"智能制造领域中外人文交流人才培养基地",教育部"中德职业教育汽车机电合作SGAVE项目"示范学校。建成"中泰国际学院""中非(乌干达)ICT学院""中德(西南)职业培训学院""中老丝路学院",推动"中文+职业技能"国际项目,成功申报中国教育部教育援外项目和重庆市国际化特色项目。

Chongqing College of Electronic Engineering insists on its internationalization orientation, and is one of the "Top 50 in world competitiveness" of higher vocational colleges, the chairman of the Chinese side of China-Africa (Chongqing) Vocational Education Union, and the only vocational college in China approved as the main and auxiliary training base for the 46th WorldSkills Competition in China with two Chinese expert group leaders. It is the talent training base for Sino-foreign cultural exchange in the field of intelligent manufacturing and a model school of Sino-German SGAVE Project for cooperation in automotive electromechanical education under the Ministry of Education. It has established China-Thailand International College, China-Africa (Uganda) ICT College and China-Germany (Southwest) Vocational Training College "China-Laos Silk Road College", and promoted "Chinese + Vocational Skills" international projects. It has successfully applied for the education aid project of the Chinese Ministry of Education and the internationalization project of Chongqing.

专业 Major

学校以专业特色统领办学特色,紧密对接重庆市"芯屏器核网"全产业链、"云联数算用"要素集群和战略性新兴产业,建有"物联网应用技术""信息安全与管理""建筑智能化"等突出电子信息和智能化特色的14个专业群,8个(专业)实体性学院以及3个(育人)功能性学院。

With its advantage of major characteristics, Chongqing College of Electronic Engineering is closely connected with the whole industrial chain of "chip-screen-network", the factor cluster of "cloud connected digital computing" and strategic emerging industries in Chongqing. It has established 14 major clusters highlighting the characteristics of electronic information and intelligence, such as Internet of Things Application Technology, Information Security and Management, Building Intelligence, etc. And it includes 8 (professional) college entities and 3 (educational) functional colleges.

建校时间 Founding time	1965年	专业 Majors	61个
教师人数 Number of teachers	1626	开学时间 Commencement time	秋季9月
学生人数 Number of students	25 016	学习年限 Years of study	3年全日制学历留学

报名联络 Registration Contact

通信地址：中国重庆市沙坪坝区大学城东路76号

邮编：401331

联系电话：86-023-65928188

联系人：国际交流与合作发展处

电子邮箱：gjhzc@cqcet.edu.cn

Address: No. 76, University City East Road, Shapingba District, Chongqing, China
Postcode: 401331
Tel: 86-023-65928188
Contact: International Exchange and Cooperation Development Division
Email: gjhzc@cqcet.edu.cn

学校介绍 School Profile

重庆公共运输职业学院
Chongqing Vocational College of Public Transportation

院校风采 Institutional Charm | 刘畅 LIU Chang

重庆公共运输职业学院副校长刘畅
LIU Chang, Vice President of Chongqing Vocational College of Public Transportation

刘畅

重庆公共运输职业学院副校长，西南轨道交通职业教育集团秘书长，分管招生就业、学生管理、校企合作、国际合作等工作。主持实施"柬埔寨职业技术创新人才培养项目"，主持教育部"2019年度教育援外项目"；主持实施"缅甸仰光省公共交通高级管理研修班""泰国高铁技术培训班"，连续5年获批重庆市政府外国留学生市长奖学金丝路项目；主持实施"走出去"企业当地人才培养网络体系建设，获重庆市国际化特色项目；主持实施"基于国有企业办职业教育、行业办学背景下推动实现毕业生高水平就业"，被遴选为重庆市典型案例；主持建设重庆市示范性职教集团，主持重庆市教育科学重点项目和教改课题5项；指导《劳动实践教育》，荣获重庆市社会实践一流课程。

Vice President of Chongqing Vocational College of Public Transportation, Secretary General of Southwest Railway Transportation Vocational Education Group, is in charge of enrollment and employment, student management, school-enterprise cooperation, international cooperation, etc. He led the implementation of "Cambodia Vocational Technology Innovation Talent Training Project", and undertook the 2019 Education Foreign Aid Project of the Ministry of Education of China. He is also responsible for the implementation of "Public Transport Senior Management Workshop in Yangon Province, Myanmar" and "Thailand High-Speed Railway Technology Training Workshop". He was awarded the Silk Road Project of Mayor Scholarship of Chongqing Municipal Government for foreign students for 5 consecutive years. The "Going out" project conducted by him for the construction of local talent training network system for enterprises was awarded the Chongqing Internationalization Project. He presided over the implementation of "Promoting high-level employment of graduates under the background of vocational education run by state-owned enterprises", which was selected as a typical case of Chongqing Municipality. He presided over the construction of Chongqing Model Vocational Education Group, and presided over 5 key projects of education science and education reform in Chongqing. He directed the research subject of *Labor Practice Education*, which won the first-class course of Chongqing Social Practice.

院校风采 | 胡兴丽
Institutional Charm | HU Xingli

重庆公共运输职业学院胡兴丽副教授
HU Xingli, Associate Professor of Chongqing Vocational College of Public Transportation

重庆公共运输职业学院交通运营教科研团队负责人，副教授，高级工程师，骨干教师，重庆市课程教学名师，主讲"城市轨道交通行车组织""城市轨道交通客运组织""城市轨道交通线路与站场"等课程。任职期间主持并参与完成多项省部级课程建设项目，其中主持并参与市级及学校教科研项目6项；公开出版专业教材4部，公开发表教科研论文8篇，其中核心论文2篇，授权实用新型专利4项；获得重庆市教学成果奖1项，校级教学成果奖2项，指导学生技能竞赛获得全国二等奖1项，市级一等奖2项，重庆市职业院校教学设计比赛市级一等奖；主持建设的"城市轨道交通行车组织"课程先后被评选为"重庆市优秀网络课程""重庆市线上线下混合式一流课程""重庆市线上一流课程"和第一批"重庆市优质课程"培育对象。

胡兴丽

Team leader of Traffic Operation Teaching and Scientific Research of Chongqing Vocational College of Public Transportation, Associate Professor, Senior Engineer, Backbone Teacher, Course Teaching Master in Chongqing. She lectures on *Urban Rail*

Transit Operation Organization, Urban Rail Transit Passenger Transport Organization,*Urban Rail Transit Lines* and *Stations* and other courses. During her tenure, she has presided over and participated in many provincial and ministerial level course construction projects, including 6 municipal and university teaching and research projects. She published 4 professional textbooks and 8 teaching and research papers, including 2 core papers and 4 authorized utility model patents. She received 1 Chongqing Teaching Achievement Award, 2 school-level Teaching Achievement Awards. Under her guidance, the students who participated in Student Skills Competition won 1 National Second Prize and 2 Municipal First Prizes. She won the Municipal First Prize in Chongqing Vocational College Teaching Design Competition. The course of "Urban Rail Transit Operation Organization" has been selected as "Chongqing Excellent Online Course", "Chongqing Online and Offline Hybrid First-Class Course", "Chongqing Online First-Class Course" and the first batch of "Chongqing High Quality Course" cultivation targets.

历史 History

重庆公共运输职业学院是一所由大型国有企业重庆城市交通开发投资（集团）有限公司全资举办的全日制交通特色高等院校。学校是重庆市最年轻的优质高职院校和高水平高职学校，拥有重庆市唯一的高水平轨道、铁道类专业群。学校是全国职工培训基地、国际铁路人才培训基地。

Chongqing Vocational College of Public Transportation is a full-time higher education institution with transportation characteristics, which is wholly owned by Chongqing City Transportation Development & Investment Group Co., Ltd, a large state-owned enterprise. It is the youngest high-quality higher vocational college and high-level higher vocational school in Chongqing, with the only high-level rail and railway major groups in Chongqing, and it is a national staff training base and an international railroad talent training base.

成就 Achievements

学校于2016年参与成立"中国—东盟轨道交通教育培训联盟"，学校是教育部中外人文交流中心智能制造领域中外人文交流人才培养基地、泰国高铁技术留学生培养基地、缅甸仰光智能交通人才培训基地、重庆市国际化特色项目建设学校。学校先后举办缅甸仰光公交高级管理研修班、中国—东盟高职院校特色合作项目、教育部教育援外项目等。学校连续4年实施重庆市人民政府外国留学生市长奖学金丝路项目，为泰国、缅甸、柬埔寨等"一带一路"沿线国家培养智能公交高级管理人才和铁道交通技术技能人才700余人。

In 2016, Chongqing Vocational College of Public Transportation participated in the establishment of the "China-ASEAN Rail Transportation Education and Training Allianc". It is a talent cultivation base for Chinese and foreign cultural exchanges in thefield of intelligent manufacturing of the China Foreign Cultural Exchange Center under the Ministry of Education, a training base for Thai students in high-speed railway technology, a talent training base for intelligent transportation of Yangon, Myanmar, and Chongqing

Internationalization Characteristic Project Construction School. Chongqing Vocational College of Public Transportation has held the senior management workshop of Yangon Public Transport in Myanmar, China-ASEAN Higher Education Institution Characteristic Cooperation Project, and Education Aid Project under the Ministry of Education, etc. For four consecutive years, it has implemented the Silk Road Project of Mayor Scholarship of Chongqing Municipal Government for Foreign Students and trained more than 700 senior intelligent bus management talents and railway transportation technical skill talents for Thailand, Myanmar, Cambodia and other countries along the "Belt and Road".

专业 Major

留学生招生重点专业：

轨道交通(城市轨道车辆运用技术、铁道机车运用与维护、动车组检修)、智慧交通(应用电子技术、人工智能技术应用、铁道信号控制)、智能装备(机械设计与制造、汽车制造及自动化、工业机器人技术、新能源汽车技术)、铁道与建筑(道路与桥梁工程技术、建设工程管理)、运输贸易(铁道交通运营管理、城市轨道交通运营管理)。

Key majors for international students:

Rail transit (application technology of urban rail vehicles, application and maintenance of railway locomotives, maintenance of electric motor train unit), Intelligent transportation (application of electronic technology, application of artificial intelligence technology, railway signal control), Intelligent equipment (mechanical design and manufacturing, automobile manufacturing and automation, industrial robot technology, new energy vehicle technology), Railway and construction (road and bridge engineering technology, construction project management), Transportation trade (railway traffic operation management, urban rail transit operation management).

建校时间 Founding time	2010年	专业 Majors	35个
教师人数 Number of teachers	500	开学时间 Commencement time	秋季9月、春季3月
学生人数 Number of students	10 000	学习年限 Years of study	1学期至3年不等

报名联络 Registration Contact

通信地址：重庆市江津区双福街道祥福大道638号
邮编：402247
联系电话：86-023-47266801　　　联系人：彭文华
电子邮箱：7127792@qq.com　　　学校网址：http://www.cqgyzy.com

Address: No. 638 Xiangfu Avenue, Shuangfu Street, Jiangjin District, Chongqing, China
Postcode: 402247
Tel: 86-023-47266801　　　Contact: Peng Wenhua
Email: 7127792@qq.com　　　Website: http://www.cqgyzy.com

学校介绍 School Profile

浙江机电职业技术学院
Zhejiang Institute of Mechanical & Electrical Engineering

院校风采 Institutional Charm | 贺星岳 HE Xingyue

浙江机电职业技术学院校长贺星岳
HE Xingyue, President of Zhejiang Institute of Mechanical & Electrical Engineering

　　七十载砥砺前行，硕果累累。1952年建校以来，学校秉承"求实、求精、求新"的校训，"开放、合作、服务"的办学理念，始终以服务浙江制造业、制造服务业为己任，致力于培养制造业以及制造服务业技能技术人才。2019年成功入选国家"双高计划"高水平学校建设单位A档(全国前十)，各项标志性成果名列全国高职院校前列。在新的历史节点上，学校踔厉奋发、笃行不怠，开启了争创特色鲜明、国内一流、国际知名的高水平职业技术大学的新征程。

Seventy years of perseverance and hard work have yielded fruitful results. Since its establishment in 1952, Zhejiang Institute of Mechanical & Electrical Engineering has adhered to the motto of

贺星岳

"seeking truth, refinement, and novelty" and the school management philosophy of "openness, cooperation, and service". It has always been committed to serving Zhejiang's manufacturing industry and manufacturing service industry, and is committed to cultivating skilled technical talents in the manufacturing industry and manufacturing service industry. In 2019, it was successfully selected as one of the A-grade (top 10 in China) high-level schools in the national "Double High-Level Plan", with its iconic achievements were among the forefront of higher vocational colleges in China. At a new historical juncture, Zhejiang Institute of Mechanical & Electrical Engineering has embarked on a new journey of striving to create a high-level vocational and technical college with distinctive characteristics, domestic first-class and internationally renowned.

山川异域，道合志同。学校积极服务"一带一路"，打造国际合作与交流平台。成功构建了"国内专科文凭+国外高级文凭"双文凭、"国内专科文凭+国际职业证书"双证书模式，形成多国别、多专业、多模式的合作办学体系。学校现有"中英伦敦南岸数字化技术联合学院""浙江丝路学院(泰国罗勇)"、缅甸教育培训服务中心、"南非智能制造培训中心""一带一路"语言与职业教育培训中心(盾安教学点)等海外教学点，诚挚欢迎世界各地的师生来校交流学习。

The mountains and rivers are different, but the paths are the same. Zhejiang Institute of Mechanical & Electrical Engineering actively serves the "the Belt and Road" and creates a platform for international cooperation and exchange. It has successfully constructed the double certificate mode of "Domestic Junior College Diploma + Foreign Higher College Diploma" and "Domestic Junior College Diploma + International Professional Certificate", forming a multi-country, multi-major and multi-model cooperative education system. Zhejiang Institute of Mechanical & Electrical Engineering now has overseas teaching sites such as Sino-British London South Bank Digital Technology Joint College, Zhejiang Silk Road College (Rayong, Thailand), Myanmar Education and Training Service Center, South Africa Intelligent Manufacturing Training Center, and the "Belt and Road" Language and Vocational Education Training Center (Dun'an Teaching Site). We warmly welcome teachers and students from all over the world to come to our school for exchange and learning.

院校风采 | 陶宇
Institutional Charm | TAO Yu

浙江机电职业技术学院国际教育学院院长陶宇
TAO Yu, Dean of International Education College of Zhejiang Institute of Mechanical & Electrical Engineering

教授，浙江机电职业技术学院国际教育学院院长；浙江省国际化特色院校建设负责人，浙江省国际学生国情教育名师，浙江省特色专业国际贸易实务专业带头人。2016年、2022年均获浙江省教学成果一等奖；2018年获世界职教院校联盟（WFCP)"高等技术技能"人才培养金奖；获得澳大利亚教师培训与评价TAE四级证书和高级培训师证书；现兼任浙江教育国际交流协会常务理

陶宇

事，浙江教育国际交流协委员会高等职业教育中外合作办学质量认证专家；浙江省高等职业教育中外合作办学项目评估专家；中国服务贸易协会专家委员会特约研究员。

Professor, Dean of International Education College of Zhejiang Institute of Mechanical & Electrical Engineering, Head of the construction of Zhejiang Internationalization Characteristic Institution, Master Teacher of national education for international students in Zhejiang Province, and Leader of International Trade Practice of Characteristic Majors in Zhejiang Province. She was awarded the Gold Award of "Higher Technical Skills" talent training by the World Federation of Colleges and Polytechnics (WFCP). She obtained Australian Teacher Training and Evaluation TAE Level 4 Certificate and Senior Trainer Certificate. She serves as the Executive Director of Zhejiang Education International Exchange Association and the Secretary General of Zhejiang Education International Exchange Association Higher Vocational Branch. she is an expert of quality certification of Sino-foreign cooperative education in higher vocational education of Sino-foreign Cooperative Education Professional Committee of China Education International Exchange Association, an expert of evaluation of Sino-foreign cooperative education projects in higher vocational education in Zhejiang Province, and a special researcher of the Expert Committee of China Association of Trade in Services.

历史 History

浙江机电职业技术学院是一所以培养机电类高素质技术技能人才为主的全日制公办高等职业院校，是国家示范性高等职业院校。学院前身是创建于1952年的杭州工人技术学校，1961年并入浙江大学，2002年成立浙江机电职业技术学院。经过70年多的建设与发展，学校已成为浙江省先进制造业紧缺人才培养的重要基地，教育部53所"国家高技能型紧缺人才培养项目"院校之一。

Zhejiang Institute of Mechanical & Electrical Engineering is a full-time public higher vocational college, which is a national model institution of higher vocational education, focusing on the cultivation of high-quality technical and skilled talents in mechanical and electrical fields. Its predecessor was Hangzhou Technical School for Workers founded in 1952, which was merged into Zhejiang University in 1961, and established as Zhejiang Institute of Mechanical & Electrical Engineering in 2002. After more than 70 years of construction and development, Zhejiang Institute of Mechanical & Electrical Engineering has become an important base for cultivating urgently-needed talents in advanced manufacturing industry in Zhejiang Province, and one of the 53 institutions of National Urgently-Needed Highly Skilled Talent Training Program under the Ministry of Education.

成就 Achievements

2015年学校被列为浙江省四年制高职教育人才培养试点学院；2016年获评首届浙江省黄炎培职业教育奖优秀学院奖和"浙江省国际化特色高校"建设单位；2017年成为浙江省重点建设高职院校；2018年荣获世界职教院校联盟(WFCP)"高等技术技能"人才培养金奖；2019年获评中国特色高水平高职学校建设单位A档（全国前十）。

Zhejiang Institute of Mechanical & Electrical Engineering was listed as a pilot college for talent training of four-year higher vocational education in Zhejiang Province in 2015, and awarded the first Zhejiang Huang Yanpei Vocational Education Award and the construction unit of "Zhejiang Internationalized Characteristic College" in 2016. In 2017, it became a key vocational college in Zhejiang Province. In 2018, it was awarded the Gold Award of "Higher Technical Skills" talent training by the World Federation of Colleges and Polytechnics (WFCP). In 2019, it was awarded the A grade construction unit (top 10 in China) of the high-level vocational colleges with Chinese characteristics.

专业 Major

招收留学生的专业：

智能制造装备技术、物联网应用技术、国际贸易实务、语言生进修项目、技能培训项目

Majors for international students:

Intelligent Manufacturing Equipment Technology, Internet of Things Application Technology, International Trade Practice, Language Refresher Program, Skills Training Program

建校时间 Founding time	1952年	专业 Majors	28个专业，80个专业方向
教师人数 Number of teachers	800	开学时间 Commencement time	秋季9月、春季3月
学生人数 Number of students	10 991	学习年限 Years of study	1年制语言进修生或者3年全日制学历留学生

报名联络 Registration Contact

通信地址： 浙江省杭州市滨江区滨文路528号

邮编： 310053

联系电话： 86-0571-87772677　　**手机：** 13735533788　　**联系人：** 孙岩松

电子邮箱： sunyansong@zime.zj.cn

学校网址： https://www.zime.edu.cn

Address: No. 528 Binwen Road, Binjiang District, Hangzhou, Zhejiang, China
Postcode: 310353
Tel: 86-0571-87772677　　Mobile: 13735533788　　Contact: Sun Yansong
Email: sunyansong@zime.zj.cn
Website: https://www.zime.edu.cn

学校介绍 School Profile

南京信息职业技术学院
Nanjing Vocational College of Information Technology

院校风采 Institutional Charm | 田敏 TIAN Min

南京信息职业技术学院校长田敏
TIAN Min, President of Nanjing Vocational College of Information Technology

　　南京信息职业技术学院是中国特色高水平高职学校、教育部优质专科高等职业院校。学校的前身是创建于1953年的南京无线电工业学校，是新中国成立后的第一所电子类中等专业学校。办学七十年来，学校为社会输送了八万余名技术技能型人才。

Nanjing Vocational College of Information Technology is a high-level vocational school with Chinese characteristics and a high-quality specialized higher vocational college under the Ministry of Education. Its predecessor was Nanjing Radio Industrial School, founded in 1953, which was the first secondary specialized school of electronics after the founding of the People's Republic of China. Over the 70 years since its establishment, Nanjing Vocational College of Information Technology has provided more than 80,000 technically skilled talents to the society.

田敏

学校主动响应"一带一路"倡议，不断进行高职教育对外开放的新探索。自2014年起，学校连续多次获得省政府来华留学奖学金支持；课程获评省级来华留学生英文授课精品课程；入选首批江苏省教育对外开放质量提升重点项目；现代通信技术专业、机电一体化技术专业分别入选首批和第二批江苏省国际化人才培养品牌专业建设项目。

The college actively responds to the "Belt and Road" initiative and continuously explores new way of opening up of higher vocational education to the outside world. Since 2014, it has received multiple provincial government scholarship support for studying in China. The course it offers has been rated as a provincial-level high-quality English teaching course for international students studying in China. It has been selected as the first batch of Jiangsu key projects to improve the quality of education opening to the outside world. And the majors of Modern Communication Technology and Mechatronics Technology have been selected as the first and second batches of brand major construction projects for international talent training in Jiangsu Province respectively.

院校风采 / Institutional Charm — 杜庆波 / DU Qingbo

南京信息职业技术学院副校长杜庆波
DU Qingbo, Vice President of Nanjing Vocational College of Information Technology

南京信息职业技术学院副校长，人工智能学院院长，二级教授，研究员级高级工程师，江苏省教学名师，工信部通信专业指导委员会副主任委员、全国铁道职业教育教学指导委员会委员、江苏省通信行业协会副理事长、南京轨道交通行业协会副理事长、"悉尼协议"应用高职联盟秘书长。

杜庆波

Vice President of Nanjing Vocational College of Information Technology, Dean of the College of Artificial Intelligence, Second-Tier Professor, Researcher Level Senior Engineer, Master teacher in Jiangsu Province, Deputy Director of the Communication Major Guidance Committee under the Ministry of Industry and Information Technology, Member of the National Railway Vocational Education Teaching Guidance Committee, Vice Chairman of the Jiangsu Communication Industry Association, Vice Chairman of the Nanjing Rail Transit Industry Association, and Secretary General of the "Sydney Agreement" Applied Higher Vocational Alliance.

历史 History

　　南京信息职业技术学院的前身是创建于1953年的南京无线电工业学校，它是新中国成立后的第一所电子类中等专业学校。3000多位外宾、专家曾到校参观交流。学校于2004年迁到仙林大学城，占地近1000亩，建筑面积38.1万平方米，现有在校生14000余人，教职工828人，其中专任教师594人。办学七十年来，学校为社会输送了八万余名技术技能型人才。

The predecessor of Nanjing Vocational College of Information Technology is Nanjing Radio Industrial School, founded in 1953, which was the first secondary specialized school of electronics after the founding of the People's Republic of China. More than 3,000 foreign guests and experts have visited the school. After its moving to Xianlin University City in 2004, it covers an area of nearly 165 acres, with a building area of 381,000 square meters. It has more than 14,000 students and 828 faculty members, including 594 full-time teachers. Over the 70 years since its establishment, it has provided more than 80,000 technically skilled talents to the society.

成就 Achievements

　　学校先后与美国、加拿大、英国、澳大利亚、韩国、新加坡、印度、芬兰、德国、新西兰、南非、越南、泰国、老挝、马来西亚、印度尼西亚等国家的高等院校和教育机构建立友好的交流关系，拓展师生境外交流学习渠道。学校是江苏省乃至华东地区较早开展学历留学生教育的高等职业院校，2014年起招收来自老挝、印度尼西亚、吉尔吉斯斯坦、埃塞俄比亚的学历留学生，与中邮建技术有限公司、埃塞俄比亚阿斯大学校企共同培养通信技术人才，2019年起承接了中南高级别人文交流机制子项目——南非学生来华学习实习项目。

Nanjing Vocational College of Information Technology has established friendly exchange relations with institutions of higher education and educational institutions in countries such as the United States, Canada, Britain, Australia, Korea, Singapore, India, Finland, Germany, New Zealand, South Africa, Vietnam, Thailand, Laos, Malaysia, Indonesia, expanding the channels for teachers and students to exchange and learn abroad. It is one of the first higher vocational colleges in Jiangsu Province and even in East China to offer education to international students with degrees. Since 2014, it has recruited foreign students with academic qualifications from Laos, Indonesia, Kyrgyzstan and Ethiopia, and jointly trained communication technology talents with China Post Construction Technology Co., Ltd. and Arsi University, Ethiopia. In 2019, it undertook the sub project of the Sino-South Africa Advanced Cultural Exchange Mechanism, a program for South African students to hold internships and study in China.

专业 Major

　　南京信息职业技术学院是中国特色高水平高职学校、国家示范性(骨干)高职院校、教育部优质专科高等职业院校、江苏省高水平高等职业院校、江苏省卓越高等职业院校培育校。学校围绕信息产品制造、信息网络、信息技术服务三大专业集群，开设43个专业，包括8个国家重点建设专业(群)、2个江苏省高校品牌专业建设工程项目、5个江苏省高水平骨干专业、3个省级品牌专业、3个省级特色专业、4个省级重点建设专业群、6个省级重点建设专业。学校建有国家级实训基地3个，省级实训基地6个，校内实验实训室215个，校外实训基地400余家。

Nanjing Vocational College of Information Technology is a high-level vocational college with Chinese characteristics, a national model (backbone) vocational college, a high-quality specialized higher vocational college under the Ministry of Education, a high-level vocational college in Jiangsu Province, and a training school of excellent higher vocational colleges in Jiangsu Province. It offers 43 majors around three major clusters of information product manufacturing, information network and information technology services, including 8 national key construction majors (clusters), 2 Jiangsu college brand major construction projects, 5 Jiangsu high-level backbone majors, 3 provincial brand majors, 3 provincial specialty majors, 4 provincial key construction major clusters and 6 provincial key construction majors. It has 3 national training bases, 6 provincial training bases, 215 on-campus experimental training rooms and more than 400 off-campus training bases.

建校时间 Founding time	1953年	专业 Majors	43个
教师人数 Number of teachers	820	开学时间 Commencement time	每年9月1日
学生人数 Number of students	14 000	学习年限 Years of study	1年预科或者3年全日制学历留学生

报名联络 Registration Contact

通信地址：南京市仙林大学城文澜路99号
邮编：210023
联系电话：86-025-85842288
电子邮箱：guojichu@njcit.cn
学校网址：https://www.njcit.cn

Address: No. 99, Wenlan Road, Xianlin University City, Nanjing, China
Post code: 210023
Contact number: 86-025-85842288
Email: guojichu@njcit.cn
Website: https://www.njcit.cn

学校介绍 School Profile

陕西能源职业技术学院
Shaanxi Energy Institute

院校风采 / 刘予东
Institutional Charm / LIU Yudong

陕西能源职业技术学院刘予东教授
LIU Yudong, Professor of Shaanxi Energy Institute

刘予东

学院始建于1953年，几经迁徙，几经更名。2023年，陕西能源职业技术学院将迎来建校七十周年。七十载栉风沐雨，风雨兼程，学院始终发扬"拼搏奉献、求实创新"的太阳石精神，十余万校友锐意进取、勤勉务实，涌现出一大批专业性人才和行业英才，在各个领域、各条战线担当作为，为中国职业教育创新发展做出积极贡献。

The college was founded in 1953, and the past years have witnessed its relocations and name changes. 2023 will mark the 70th anniversary of Shaanxi Energy Institute. Over the past 70 years of hardships, the college has always carried forward the Sunstone Spirit of "perseverance, dedication, practicality, and innovation", producing more than 100,000 alumni who are enterprising, diligent, and pragmatic. These alumni have emerged as a large number of professional and industry elites, making positive contributions to the innovation and development of vocational education in China in various fields and on various fronts.

在长期的发展中,"敬学、明德、远志、修能"的校训激发了学校改革发展的蓬勃生机与不竭动力。学校先后成为省级示范性高职院校、国家优质专科高等职业院校,2019年被确定为中国特色高水平专业群建设单位、2022年获批成为陕西省高水平高职学校建设单位,实现学校发展历史性的新跃升。我们将踔厉奋发,奋勇向前,开启陕西能源职业技术学院"双高建设"和高质量发展新征程!

In its long-term development, with the motto of "Respecting learning, Cultivating morality, Aspiring far, and Enhancing ability", Shaanxi Energy Institute has made vigorous advancement with inexhaustible vitality and power. It has successively become a provincial model vocational college, a national high-quality specialized higher vocational college. In 2019, it was designated as a high-level construction unit of major cluster with Chinese characteristics. In 2022, it was approved as a high-level construction unit of vocational college in Shaanxi Province, achieving a historic leap in its development. We will forge ahead with determination and courage, embarking on a new journey of "Double High-Level Plan" construction and high-quality development.

院校风采 赵新法
Institutional Charm ZHAO Xinfa

陕西能源职业技术学院赵新法教授
ZHAO Xinfa, Professor of Shaanxi Energy Institute

二级教授,陕西普通高等学校教学名师,全国煤炭行业职业教育煤炭综合加工利用类专业带头人,煤炭行业技能人才工作特别贡献人员奖获得者,咸阳市第八批有突出贡献的专家;现任学院双高建设专家咨询委员会常务副主任,兼任陕西省煤炭工业协会副会长,陕西省煤炭学会副理事长;曾公开发表科研论文39篇,主持完成职业教育国家教学成果二等奖1项、全国煤炭行业教育教学成果特等奖1项;主持完成陕西省高职教育煤化工技术专业教学资源库建设、能源类省级创新创业教育培训基地创建以及学院化工类专业的省级重点专业、综合改革试点、精品课程、教学团队以及石化行业教学团队项目建设;主持完成教育部《高等职业教育资源环境与安全大类专业教学标准开发规程研究》《煤化工技术专业教学标准》研制;主编全国煤炭高职高

赵新法

专规划教材《化学》《煤化学》；参与教育部《煤炭行业人才需求与专业设置指导报告》编制工作。

Second-Tier professor, Master teacher of Shaanxi colleges and universities, Academic leader in the comprehensive processing and utilization of coal in the national coal industry vocational education, Winner of the Special Contributor Award for skilled talents in the coal industry, and one of the eighth batch of experts with outstanding contributions in Xianyang, Shaanxi. Currently, he serves as the Executive Deputy Director of the Expert Advisory Committee for the "Double High-Level Construction" of the college, the Vice President of the Shaanxi Coal Industry Association and the Vice Chairman of the Shaanxi Coal Association. He has published 39 scientific research papers, won the second prize of National Teaching Achievements for Vocational Education and the special prize of National Coal Industry Education Teaching Achievements. He presided over the construction of the teaching resource database for the coal chemical technology major in Shaanxi vocational education, the creation of a provincial-level innovation and entrepreneurship education training base in energy category, and the construction of provincial-level key majors, comprehensive reform pilot projects, high-quality courses, teaching teams, and petrochemical industry teaching team of Chemical Engineering major in the college. He also led the *Research on the Development Regulations of Teaching Standards for Higher Vocational Education Resource Environment and Safety Maior,* and the *Formulation of Teaching Standards for CoaChemical Technology Major,* He is the editor-in-chief of the national coal vocational high school and college plannintextbooks such as *Chemistry* and *Coal Chemistry.* He participated in the preparation of the *Guidance Report on TalentDemand and Maior Setting in the Coal industry* under the Ministry of Education.

历史 History

陕西能源职业技术学院其前身创建于1953年，是一所由陕西省人民政府创办的全日制普通高等职业院校。2001年，经陕西省人民政府批准，原国家级重点中专陕西煤炭工业学校、省部级重点中专西安煤炭卫生学校和陕西煤炭职工大学合并组建成陕西能源职业技术学院。它起初隶属于陕西省煤炭生产安全监督管理局，2011年划转由陕西省教育厅管理。60多年来，学校坚持以服务为宗旨、以就业为导向、走工学结合的特色发展道路，坚持"质量立院、人才强院、特色铸院、创新兴院、依法治院"的办学理念，形成全日制教育、继续教育、安全培训等多层次、多形式的职业教育办学格局。

Shaanxi Energy Institute is a full-time ordinary higher vocational college founded by Shaanxi Provincial Government, with its predecessor established in 1953. In 2001, with the approval of Shaanxi Provincial Government, the former national key technical secondary school Shaanxi Coal Industry School, provincial and ministerial key technical secondary school Xi'an Coal Medical School and Shaanxi Coal Workers' College were merged into Shaanxi Energy Institute. It initially belonged to the Shaanxi Provincial Coal Production Safety Supervision and Administration Bureau, and was transferred to the administration of Shaanxi Provincial Education Department in 2011. For more than 60 years, the school has adhered to the characteristic development path of combining job and learning with the orientation of service and employment, and insisted on the educational philosophy of "establishing the school with quality, strengthening the school with talents, casting the school with characteristics, prospering the school with innovation, and governing the school according to law", forming a multi-level and multi-form vocational education pattern of full-time education, continuing education, and safety training.

专业 Major

拟开展留学生招收的意向专业：

煤矿智能开采技术、煤炭清洁利用技术、康复治疗技术、护理

The majors that we are proposing to offer to international students are:

Intelligent Coal Mining Technology, Coal Clean Utilization Technology, Rehabilitation Therapy Technology, Nursing.

建校时间 Founding time	1953年	专业 Majors	50个专业（包括1个电气自动化本科专业）
教师人数 Number of teachers	732	开学时间 Commencement time	秋季9月、春季3月
学生人数 Number of students	18 000余	学习年限 Years of study	3年或5年

报名联络 Registration Contact

通信地址：陕西省咸阳市文林路29号

医学校区：陕西省西安市平峪路88号

邮编：712000

办公室电话：86-029-33665111； 33665222

招生咨询电话：86-029-33665101； 33665102； 33665103

传真：86-029-33665100

学校网址：http://www.sxny.cn

招生网址：http://www.sxny.cn

Address: No. 29, Wenlin Road, Xianyang City, Shaanxi, China
Medical Campus: No.88 Pingyu Road, Xi'an, Shaanxi, China
Postcode: 712000
Tel: 86-029-33665111； 33665222
Enrollment Consultation Tel: 86-029-33665101； 33665102； 33665103
Fax: 86-029-33665100
School website: http://www.sxny.cn
Enrollment website: http://www.sxny.cn

学校介绍 School Profile

北京经济管理职业学院
Beijing Institute of Economics and Management

院校风采 Institutional Charm | **田宏忠** TIAN Hongzhong

北京经济管理职业学院院长田宏忠
TIAN Hongzhong, President of Beijing Institute of Economics and Management

田宏忠

四十多年风雨沧桑，北京经济管理职业学院走过了一条求索、创新、奋斗之路，由一所起步维艰的成人培训学校发展成为国内外颇具影响力的高职院校。

Over the past more than 40 years of ups and downs, Beijing Institute of Economics and Management has gone through a path of exploration, innovation, and striving, evolving from a struggling adult training school into a highly influential vocational college at home and abroad.

北京经济管理职业学院是北京市人民政府批准、教育部备案、北京市教育委员会主管的公办全日制普通高等职业学院。学校成立于1979年，现有北京望京和河北固安两个校区，国际化设施条件完备，专业性师资队伍齐全。学校按照"高质量、有特色、国际化"的办学要求，积极适应国家及北京职业人才需求，优化调整学生培养方案、加强数字化课程建设，学校就业率达98%以上。

Beijing Institute of Economics and Management is a public full-time ordinary higher vocational college approved by Beijing Municipal Government, registered with the Ministry of Education, and supervised by the Beijing Municipal Education Commission. The school was established in 1979 and currently has two campuses of Wangjing in Beijing and Gu'an in Hebei province, with fully equipped international facilities and a professional teaching staff. In accordance with the requirements of "high quality, distinctiveness, and internationalization", the school actively adapts to the needs of vocational talents in the country and Beijing, optimizes and adjusts student training programs and strengthens digital course construction, achieving a graduate employment rate of over 98%.

未来，"改革"将成为北京经济管理职业学院永远不变的底色，厚德强技、知行合一、奋斗为本、事业为上的经管精神将愈加历久弥新。

In the future, "reform" will remain the constant theme of Beijing Institute of Economics and Management, and the management spirit of being virtuous, strong in skill, integrating knowledge and action, striving for excellence, and putting career first will continue to be renewed.

历史 History

北京经济管理职业学院办学历史溯源于1979年成立的北京市经委职工教育师资进修学校，1984年更名为北京市经济管理干部学院，2003年原国家经贸委在学校挂牌成立北京经理学院。2006年，学校转制为普通高等学校，更名为北京经济管理职业学院。2012年10月，学校隶属关系由市国资委转至市教委。

The history of Beijing Institute of Economics and Management is traced back to the Beijing Municipal Economic and Trade Commission Staff Education and Teacher Training School which was established in 1979 and renamed in 1984 as Beijing Institute of Economic Management Cadres. In 2003, the former State Economic and Trade Commission established Beijing Management College in the school. In 2006, the school was transformed into a general higher education institution and renamed as Beijing Institute of Economics and Management. In October 2012, the affiliation of the school was transferred from the Municipal State-owned Assets Supervision and Administration Commission to Beijing Municipal Education Commission.

学校特色 School Features

北京经济管理职业学院是北京市人民政府批准、教育部备案、北京市教育委员会主管的公办全日制普通高等职业学院。学校可以招收学历留学生的学院包括临空经济管理学院、数字财金学院、人工智能学院、外语与学前教育学院、珠宝与艺术设计学院、培训学院。

Beijing Institute of Economics and Management is a public full-time ordinary higher vocational college approved by Beijing Municipal Government, registered with the Ministry of Education, and supervised by the Beijing Municipal Education Commission. The College of Beijing Institute of Economics and Management that can enroll international students with academic qualifications include College of Airport Economics and Management, College of Digital Finance and Accounting, College of Artificial Intelligence, College of Foreign Languages and Pre-College Education, College of Jewelry and Art Design, and College of Continuing Education.

1. 临空经济管理学院

临空经济管理学院是国内首个以临空经济为特色的专业群学院，开设中央财政支持重点专业国际商务、跨境电子商务，国家级示范专业旅游管理，特色专业空中乘务，传统优势专业工商企业管理，新兴热点专业休闲服务与管理。学院建设有北京市特色高水平骨干专业群和实训基地——"临空经济管理专业群""京东国际数字贸易工程师学院""李浩国际餐饮艺术设计大师工作室"。学院师资力量雄厚，教师团队入选教育部课程思政教学名师和教学团队。学院获得中国国际"互联网+"大学生创新创业大赛国赛银奖1项，铜奖4项，"中英'一带一路'国际青年创新创业大赛"世界赛金银奖牌共4块，并代表中国赴英交流竞技。学院通过数字赋能、产教融合，培养新时代的"国门工匠"。

College of Airport Economics and Management is the first dedicated college in China that establishes a major cluster related to airport economy. Programs offered at the College include: International Business, Cross-border E-commerce, two programs receiving key funding support from central government; Tourism Management, a national demonstrative program; Flight Attendant, a distinctive program of the College; Business Administration, a competitive program of the College; and Leisure Service and Management, an emerging and popular program in recent years."Airport Economics and Management Major Cluster", "JD Institute for International Digital Trade Engineer", "Li Hao International Catering Art Design Master Studio" are Characteristic and High-level Key Major Cluster and Practice Base of Beijing Municipality. The College boasts experienced and professional teachers, and its teaching team has been selected as Famous Teachers and Teaching Team of Ideological Education by the Ministry of Education. The College has won one silver award and four bronze awards of the National Competition of China International College Students' "Internet+"Innovation and Entrepreneurship Competition, won four gold medals and silver medals in the World Competition of "China-UK 'B&R' International Youth Innovation and Enterprise Skills Competition", and went to UK for exchanges and competitions on behalf of China. The College is devoted to cultivating "national craftsman" for the new era through digital empowerment and industry-education integration.

2. 数字财金学院

数字财金学院开设大数据与会计、财税大数据应用、金融服务与管理、金融科技应用等专业。学院服务北京"四个中心"建设，契合北京建设全球数字经济标杆城市战略，积极推动专业数字化升级，同时努力实现职业教育国际化，取得了标志性成果。数字财金专业群会计专业为北京市中澳合作TAFE项目试点改革专业；开发了系列中英双语课程"投资中国""中外财务报表比较分析"等，其中"投资中国"入选英国雷丁大学亨利商学院学士学位课程；出版了《金融科技》英文版教材；与利安达国际会计网络开展校企合作；承办第三届全球数字经济大会分论坛：全球数字财金发展与技能人才培养专题论坛，向世界推广中国的职业教育。

College of Digital Finance offers such programs as Big Data and Accounting, Application of Financial and Tax Big Data, Financial Service and Management, and Application of Financial Technology. Committed to the building of "four centers" of Beijing Municipality, the College contributes its part in Beijing's strategy to build the capital as a global benchmark city for digital economy by promoting digital upgrading of majors while facilitating internationalization of vocational education with iconic achievements. Accounting in digital finance major cluster is a pilot reform major under China-Australia TAFE Program of Beijing Municipality. The College developed bilingual courses in Chinese and English: "Invest in China", "Comparative Analysis on Financial Statements Between China and Other Countries" with the former being selected as bachelor degree course of Henley Business School of University of Reading. It published an English textbook *Financial Technology*, conducted school-enterprise cooperation with Reanda International, and hosted Global Digital Economy Conference 2023: Global Digital Finance Development and Skilled Talents Cultivation Forum to promote China's vocational education to the world.

3. 人工智能学院

人工智能学院现有大数据技术、人工智能技术应用、信息安全技术应用、工程造价、电气自动化技术以及智能机电技术专业。其中人工智能技术应用是北京市高职第一所教育部人工智能学院建设专业；是第一个北京市重点建设的人工智能专业群核心专业，是第一个人工智能应用专业北京市"双师型"教师培养培训基地；拥有第一个国家级的"人工智能技术应用"教学创新团队。专业依托北京市特色高水平工程师学院、科大讯飞、商汤、百度等头部企业的技术优势，对接数据处理工程师、人工智能训练师、智能系统运维工程师、售前售后技术支持、人工智能产品经理等岗位培养高素质技术技能型人才。

College of Artificial Intelligence currently offers programs such as Big Data Technology, Application of Artificial Intelligence Technology, Application of Information Security Technology, Engineering Cost, Electric Automation Technology, and Intelligent Electromechanical Technology. Application of Artificial Intelligence Technology is the first artificial intelligence major among vocational colleges of Beijing Municipality approved by the Ministry of Education, the first key major in AI major cluster of Beijing Municipality, and the first dual-role teacher training base for Application of Artificial Intelligence of Beijing Municipality. Application of Artificial Intelligence Technology is the first national level teaching innovation team. Tapping into the technological advantages of Characteristic and High-level Engineer College of Beijing Municipality, iFLYTEK, SenseTime, Baidu, and other leading companies, the College cultivate high-quality and skilled talents to work as data processing engineer, AI trainer, engineer for intelligent system operation and maintenance, specialist for pre-sales and after-sales technical service, and AI product manager.

4. 外语与学前教育学院

外语与学前教育学院打造的国际教育服务专业群于2021年成功入选北京市第三批职业院校特色高水平骨干专业群。立足服务北京"国际交往中心"功能定位，服务高质量民生，国际教育服务专业群以商务英语（教育服务）、应用英语（双语教育）、学前教育三个专业有机协同发展，培养"精英语、懂教育、会管理、有特长"的国际化高素质复合型技术技能人才。作为教育部职业院校外语类专业教学指导委员会委员单位、北京市高教学会大学英语研究分会职业英语专委会会长单位，承担多项国家级、市级项目如高等职业院校专业目录、简介和专业教学标准的修（制）订工作。

International education service major cluster by College of Foreign Languages and Pre-school Education was selected into the third batch of Characteristic and High-level Key Major Clusters of Beijing Municipality in 2021. Targeted at Beijing's goal to build the city as an international exchange center and to contribute to people's well-being, the College promotes coordinated development of Business English (educational service), Applied English (bilingual education), and Pre-school Education in international education service major cluster to cultivate international, high-quality, compound, and skilled talents who master English, understand education, know management, and have their own strong points. As a member unit of MOE Teaching Steering Committee for Language Majors of Vocational Schools and a chair unit of Vocational English Committee under College English Research Sub-committee of Beijing Association of Higher Education, the College undertakes several national and municipal projects such as compilation and revision of major catalogue and introduction of vocational colleges and teaching standards.

5. 珠宝与艺术设计学院

珠宝与艺术设计学院设宝玉石鉴定与加工（周大福订单班）、玉器设计与工艺、工艺美术品设计、数字媒体技术（北京卫视订单班）4个专业。出版《玉器工艺》系列化国际中英双语教材，制定工艺美术专业人才培养方案（英文版），形成国际化专业人才培养"经管方案"；完成《1+X贵金属首饰制作与检验证书国际化路径研究》课题；筹建巴基斯坦瓜达尔港丝路学堂（珠宝艺术学院分院）；入选坦桑尼亚珠宝加工技术员4-5级国家职业标准开发项目；连续两年面向全球五百多名留学生完成教育部"汉语桥"项目。打造基于产教融合的"数字+非遗技艺传创"全国珠宝首饰与非遗技艺传承"北京范式"、全国珠宝与艺术设计师资培养的"北京基地"、面向国际传播中华优秀宝玉石文化的"北京频道"。

College of Jewellery and Art Design offers the four programs of Jewellery Appraisal and Processing (Chow Tai Fook Order Class), Jadeware Design and Crafts, Arts and Crafts Design, and Digital Media Technology (Order Class of Beijing Radio and Television Network). The College published bilingual textbook *Jadeware Crafts* in Chinese and English, formulated the English version of *1+X Precious Metal Jewellery Making and Path for International Recognition of Inspection Certificate* cultivation plan for arts and crafts talents, and established a BIEM plan for cultivation of international professionals. It finished Research on, established Silk Road School(Sub-branch of College of Jewellery and Art Design) at Gwadar Port of Pakistan, and was included in Tanzanian National Vocational Standard Development Project for Level 4 to 5 Jewellery Processing Technicians. The College delivered MOE "Chinese Bridge" for more than 500 overseas students from across the globe. It is devoted to developing a "Beijing model" based on industry-education integration that "combines digital means with inheritance and innovation of intangible crafts" for jewellery and intangible crafts, building a "Beijing base" for cultivation of jewellery and art designer, and a" Beijing channel" to promote excellent jewellery culture of China to the world.

6. 培训学院

培训学院自1989年开始留学生汉语培训，截至目前，已有112个国家和地区的17 000余名国际学生在我校学习。我校立足职业教育新发展阶段，贯彻"中文+职业技能"新发展理念，依托优势专业，服务"一带一路"，将优秀文化传播、汉语培训、专业能力提升和实践技能培训有机结合，构建课内课外贯通、线上线下融合的国际学生培养模式。2017年，学校荣获全国高职院校"国际影响力50强"。2020、2021年连续两年获得泰国教育部职业教育委员会颁发的"中泰职业教育国际合作突出贡献奖"。

Training College started Chinese language training for overseas students in 1989. As of now, more than17,000 students from 112 countries and regions have studied Chinese at BIEM. For the new development phase of vocational education, BIEM follows the new development philosophy of "combining Chinese and vocational skills", gives full expression to its advantages in competitive majors, and contributes to the "Belt and Road" Initiative. Integrating promotion of excellent culture, Chinese language training, professional capability improvement,and skill training,

BIEM established a cultivation model for international students that covers in-class and after-class activities through virtual and in-person ways. In 2017, BIEM was awarded Top 50 Vocational Colleges in terms of international influence. In 2020 and 2021, it was granted China-Thailand Vocational Education International Cooperation Outstanding Cooperation Award by the Office of Vocational Education Commission, Ministry of Education, Thailand.

专业 Major

拟开展留学生招收的意向专业：

临空经济管理学院：工商企业管理；国际商务

数字财金学院：大数据与会计；金融服务与管理（银行方向）

人工智能学院：信息安全技术应用（奇虎360信息安全订单班）；人工智能技术应用（科大讯飞人工智能工程师学院班）

外语与学前教育学院：商务英语

珠宝与艺术设计学院：宝玉石鉴定与加工（智慧运营方向）；工艺美术品设计

培训学院：中文培训

The majors that we are proposing to offer to international students are:

College of Airport Economics and Management：Business Administration；International Business

College of Digital Finance：Big Data and Accounting; Financial Services and Management (Banking)

College of Artificial Intelligence：Information Security Technology Application (Qihoo 360 Information Security Order Class)；Application of Artificial Intelligence Technology (IFlytek DAI Engineer Class)

College of Foreign Languages and Pre-School Education：Business English

College of Jewellry and Art Design：Gemstone Identification and Processing (intelligent operation)；Arts and Crafts Design

College of Continuing Education：Chinese Language

建校时间 Founding time	1979年	专业 Majors	24个专科专业
教师人数 Number of teachers	498	开学时间 Commencement time	秋季9月、春季3月
学生人数 Number of students	3000余	学习年限 Years of study	1学期至3年不等

【录取条件】

申请条件

1. 品德良好，无犯罪记录及其他不良信用记录的外籍人士
2. 持有效护照且身体健康
3. 具有高中毕业证书
4. HSK4级及以上证书
5. 有可靠的经济保证和在华事务担保人

*奖学金介绍：学校为成绩优异的学生提供全额或半额奖学金。

Application conditions

1. Foreigners with good moral character, no criminal record and other bad credit records.
2. Holding a valid passport and in good health.
3. Possessing a high school graduation certificate.
4. HSK4 level or above certificates.
5. Having reliable financial guarantee and guarantor for affairs in China.

* The school offers full or half scholarships for students with excellent academic performance.

报名联络 Registration Contact

报名时间：
每年12月至次年5月31日

Registration time:
From December to May 31 of the following year.

联系方式：

通信地址：北京市朝阳区花家地街12号

邮编：100020

学校网址：https://www.biem.edu.cn

联系电话：86-010-8417-1004

电子邮箱：iec@biem.edu.cn

Address: No. 12 Huajiadi Street, Chaoyang District, Beijing, China
Postcode Code: 100020
Website: https://www.biem.edu.cn
Tel: 86-010-8417-1004
Email: iec@biem.edu.cn

职教名校申请手册

学校介绍 School Profile

重庆工程职业技术学院
Chongqing Vocational Institute of Engineering

院校风采 Institutional Charm — 张进 ZHANG Jin

重庆工程职业技术学院院长张进教授
ZHANG Jin, President of Chongqing Vocational Institute of Engineering

"凿开混沌得乌金，蓄藏阳和意最深。"（于谦《咏煤炭》）

重庆工程职业技术学院以"应时之所需，急家国之用，育技能之才"的办学理念深耕职教改革发展70余年，立足能源办学特色，抢抓智慧物联机遇，自强土木测绘优势，从一所煤炭行业学校发展成为一所工科优势突出、行业特色鲜明、多学科渗透相融、多元协调开放的中国高职教育名校。

"Chiseling through chaotic strata to obtain coal, which holds endless heat and deep affection." (From *Ode to the Coal* by Yu Qian)

For over 70 years, Chongqing Vocational Institute of Engineering has been deeply engaged in vocational education reform and development with the educational philosophy of "meeting the needs of the time, serving the urgent needs of the nation, and cultivating skilled talents". Based on its characteristic education

张进

in energy, the institute has seized the opportunities of smart IOT, and strengthened its advantages in civil engineering and surveying, transforming from a coal industry school to a leading vocational college in China with its outstanding engineering, distinctive industry characteristics, multidisciplinary integration, and diverse coordination and openness.

在实现教育现代化、加快建成教育强国的关键时期，重庆工程职业技术学院将继续守正创新，开放进取，努力为推进区域产业的高质量发展培养具有"砺苦、谨信、惟精、弘毅"特质的高层次技术技能人才，将"渝工程"打造成为国内一流、国际知名的职业院校，在深化职业教育改革发展的大潮中更上一层楼。

During the critical period of China's achieving modern education and accelerating the construction of an education power, Chongqing Vocational Institute of Engineering will continue to be innovative, open-minded, and strive to cultivate high-level technical talents with the qualities of "perseverance, trustworthiness, excellence, and fortitude" to promote the high-quality development of regional industries. It aims to build the "Chongqing Project" into a nationally first class and internationally famous vocational college, and make further progress in the tide of deepening the reform and development of vocational education.

历史 History

学校建于1951年，有72年的历史，是一所由重庆市人民政府举办，重庆市教育委员会主管的全日制普通高等职业学校、国家建设类技能型紧缺人才培养试点高校、国家示范性高等职业院校和中国特色高水平专业建设计划学校。校园占地近1300亩，现有全日制专科在校学生17 000余人，年平均培养长短期国际学生200余人。学校开设有57个专科（高职）专业。现有教职工1000余人，国际化师资100余人。

Founded in 1951, Chongqing Vocational Institute of Engineering has a history of 72 years. It is a full-time general higher vocational school organized by the Chongqing Municipal Government and supervised by the Chongqing Municipal Education Commission. It is also a national pilot institute for cultivating urgently needed skilled talents, a National Demonstrative Higher Vocational College, and a High Level Vocational Institute with Chinese Characteristics and Specialized Construction Plan. Its campus covers an area of nearly 1300 Chinese Mu, with over 17,000 full-time college students and over 200 long-term and short-term international students cultivated here each year. The institute offers 57 specialized (vocational) majors. There are currently more than 1,000 staff, including over 100 international teachers.

成就 Achievements

学校办学历史久远，强调开放性教育，与泰国、马来西亚、老挝、俄罗斯、乌兹别克斯坦、白俄罗斯等"一带一路"沿线20余国开展海外留学生培养、技术服务以及合作举办中外合作办学机构。

Chongqing Vocational Institute of Engineering has a long history. It emphasizes open education and has conducted overseas student training, technical services and cooperation in organizing Sino-foreign institutions with more than 20 countries along the Belt and Road, including Thailand, Malaysia, Laos, Russia, Uzbekistan and Belarus.

学院是中泰职教联盟中方理事长单位，教育部鲁班工坊建设联盟副理事长单位，中国国际教育交流协会职业技术教育国际交流分会第二届理事会副理事长单位，教育部"未来非洲–中非职教合作计划"中非应用型人才联合培养子项目课程建设组秘书处。成功入选世界职业院校与技术大学联盟卓越奖，全国首批20个"中国–东盟高职院校特色合作项目"院校，"高等职业院校国际影响力50强"，重庆市国际化特色项目等。

The institute is the Chairman of the Chinese side of the China-Thailand Vocational Education Alliance, Vice President of the Luban Workshop Construction Union under the Ministry of Education, Vice President of the second council of Vocational and Technical Education International Exchange Branch under China International Education Exchange Association, and Secretariat of the curriculum construction group of the China-Africa Joint Training Sub-program for Applied Talents under the "Future of Africa - China-Africa TVET" program of the Ministry of Education. It has been awarded the Silver Prize of the World Federation of Colleges and Polytechnics. It's also one of the first 20 selected colleges of China-ASEAN Successful TVET Cooperative Program, one of the "Top 50 Institutions of Higher Vocational Education with International Influence", and one of the selected in Chongqing Internationalization Specialized Program, etc.

专业 Major

留学生招生重点专业：

现代移动通信技术、机电一体化技术、物联网应用技术、建筑工程技术、旅游管理

Key majors for international students:

Modern Mobile Communication Technology, Machine Electrical Integration Technology, Internet of Things Application Technology, Architectural Engineering Technology, Tourism Management.

建校时间 Founding time	1951年	专业 Majors	50个
教师人数 Number of teachers	1000余	开学时间 Commencement time	秋季9月、春季3月
学生人数 Number of students	17 000	学习年限 Years of study	1年预科或者3年全日制学历

报名联络 Registration Contact

通信地址：中国重庆市江津区圣泉街道南北大道南段1111号

邮编：402260

联系电话：86-023-61065970

电子邮箱：cqviegjxy@cqvie.edu.cn　　学校网址：https://www.cqvie.edu.cn

Address: No.1111 south section of Nanbei Ave, Shengquan Street. Jiangjin District, Chongqing, China
Postcode: 402260
Tel: 86-023-61065970
Email: cqviegjxy@cqvie.edu.cn　　Website: https://www.cqvie.edu.cn

学校介绍 School Profile

潍坊职业学院
Weifang Vocational College

院校风采 Institutional Charm | 刘建成 LIU Jiancheng

潍坊职业学院校领导刘建成
LIU Jiancheng, Leader of Weifang Vocational College

潍坊职业学院秉承"明德尚学、强能善技"的校训精神，践行"崇实尚行、敢于争先"的潍职精神，致力于打造"引领改革、支撑发展、中国特色、世界水平"的高职院校，经过60余年积累与发展，各项工作取得令人瞩目的成就。学院是全国优质专科高等职业院校、中国特色高水平高职学校和专业建设计划建设单位，连续3年获评山东省高职院校办学质量考核第一名，为区域经济社会发展培养了大批高素质技术技能人才。

Weifang Vocational College (WFVC) has adhered to the school motto of "exposing virtues, pursing knowledge, strengthening capabilities and polishing skills" and practiced the spirit of "honoring truth and practice, and striving to be the first". WFVC has been committed to

刘建成

building a world-level higher vocational college with Chinese characteristics that leads educational reform and supports the development of society. We have made remarkable achievements after over 60 years of development and trained a large number of highly qualified technical talents for regional economic and social development. It is a National High-quality Vocational College of Higher Education and a member of the High-level Vocational Colleges and Majors Construction Plan for Preserving Chinese Characteristics. It ranked first in the quality assessment of higher vocational colleges in Shandong for three consecutive years.

院校风采 / Institutional Charm — 丁世民 DING Shimin

潍坊职业学院丁世民教授
DING Shimin, Professor of Weifang Vocational College

丁世民

国家"万人计划"教学名师，二级教授，园林技术国家级教师教学创新团队核心成员，主持国家级职业教育教学成果二等奖1项、首届教材建设奖二等奖1项、省级及以上教科研项目20余项。具有36年的园林技术一线工作经验，提出教学与社会服务"双线融合"的课程改革理念，将企业真实案例和社会服务项目动态融入课程教学，建成1门国家级精品资源共享课程，1门省级精品在线开放课程，配套开发2本"十三五"职业教育国家规划教材，主持的《园林植物保护》课程在国家智慧教育公共服务平台、中国大学慕课等平台上线，服务各类学习者累计2万余人；组建园林植物养护团队，利用潍坊职业农民学院等平台，每年开展高素质农民培训1万余人次，助力乡村振兴。

Professor of the national "Ten Thousand Talents Plan" and a core member of garden technology national teaching innovation team. He has won the second prize of national vocational education teaching achievement, the second prize of first textbook construction award and presided over more than 20 teaching and research projects of provincial and national level. Enjoying 36-year teaching experience in garden technology, he has put forward the curriculum reform concept of "integration of teaching and social service" and added the enterprise real cases and dynamic social service projects into curriculum teaching. He has established one state-level high-quality sharing course, one provincial high-quality online open course, and completed two textbooks of vocational education national planning for the 13th Five-Year Plan. The course of Garden Plant Protection presided over by him is available on the platforms such as Smart Education of China and MOOC, which has served a total of more than 20,000 learners. He has set up a team of garden plant maintenance and provided more than 10,000 high-quality farmer training opportunities each year at Weifang Vocational Farmer College to help rural revitalization.

历史 History

潍坊职业学院是2001年7月经山东省人民政府批准组建的公办全日制普通高职院校，始建于1956年，学院坚持面向市场、服务发展、促进就业的办学方向，经过60余年的积累与发展，形成了专业建设与区域产业相融合、人才培养过程与生产实践相融合、学院文化与企业文化相融合，学院发展对接区域经济社会发展的"三融合一对接"办学特色，为区域经济社会发展培养了大批高素质技术技能人才。学校坐落在著名的世界风筝都、中国优秀旅游城市——山东省潍坊市，现有奎文和滨海两个校区。2014年开展留学生教育，至今已有来自20多个国家和地区的1000余名留学生来校学习。

WFVC is a public full-time higher vocational college approved by People's Government of Shandong Province in 2001. Established in 1956, the College adheres to the principles of orienting towards market, development and employment. During more than 60 years of history, WFVC has focused on running the school by connecting local industries, production practice and enterprise cultures, and trained a large number of high-quality technical and skilled talents for regional economic and social development. WFVC is located in the city of Weifang, Shandong Province, the famous World's Kite Capital and a national tourism city. There are two campuses of Kuiwen and Binhai. More than 1,000 international students from over 20 countries and regions have come to study at WFVC since 2014.

成就 Achievements

潍坊职业学院是中国特色高水平高职学校和专业建设计划建设单位，入选全国高职院校"教学资源50强""服务贡献50强""国际影响力50强""综合竞争力100强"；连续3年获评山东省高职院校办学质量考核第一名。学院持续推进国际化发展战略，举办"未来非洲""汉语桥""网络中文课堂""中文工坊"等项目，形成独具特色的"留学潍职"教育品牌，连续三年荣获全国高等职业院校"国际影响力50强"。

WFVC is a member of the High-level Vocational Colleges and Majors Construction Programs for Preserving Chinese Characteristics. It ranks in the Top 50 categories of Higher Vocational Colleges in "Teaching Resources","Service Contribution" and "International Influence" and Top 100 of Comprehensive Competitiveness. It ranked first in the quality assessment of higher vocational colleges in the Province of Shandong for three consecutive years,The college continues to promote the internationalization development strategy, organizes "Future Africa", "Chinese Bridge", "Online Chinese Classroom" and "Center for Chinese Language Professional Skills", etc. Forming a uniqne "Study in WFVC" education brand, WFVC won the honor "Top 50 Colleges of International Influence"for three consecutive years.

专业 Major

学校设有"3+2"分段培养本科专业3个，高职专业51个。

国际学生招生：语言预科生、学历生；

招收国际学生的学历专业：机电一体化技术、国际商务、旅游管理、计算机应用技术、电子商务和园艺技术等；

奖学金情况：现设有省政府奖学金和校奖学金。

WFVC offers three "3+2" undergraduate programs and 51 higher vocational diploma programs.
We welcome international students to study language preparatory courses and diploma programs.
The diploma programs for international students includes Mechatronics Technology, Tourism Management, Computer Application Technology, E-Commerce and Horticulture Technology.
Provincial government scholarships and college scholarships are available.

建校时间 Founding time	1956年	专业 Majors	本科3个、高职51个
教师人数 Number of teachers	1078	开学时间 Commencement time	秋季9月、春季3月
学生人数 Number of students	20 000	学习年限 Years of study	1学年至4年不等

报名联络　Registration Contact

通信地址：山东省潍坊市东风东街8029号

邮编：261041

联系电话：86-0536-5135939

联系人刘老师（英语）微信：18053610638

联系人韩老师（俄语）微信：15908000091

电子邮箱：wzgjch@163.com；gjjyxy@sdwfvc.edu.cn

学校网址：http://www.sdwfvc.com

Address: No. 8029, Dongfeng East Street, Weifang, Shandong, China
Postcode: 261041
Tel: 86-0536-5135939
Contact:
Ms. Liu (English)　WeChat: 18053610638
Mr. Han (Russian)　WeChat: 15908000091
Email: wzgjch@163.com; gjjyxy@sdwfvc.edu.cn
Website: http://www.sdwfvc.com

学校介绍 School Profile

北京工业职业技术学院
Beijing Polytechnic College

历史 History

北京工业职业技术学院地处北京市石景山区，是一所由北京市政府举办的普通高等职业院校，是全国首批独立设置的高职院校、国家示范高职院校、全国高等职业院校校长联席会主席团单位。学校前身为创建于1956年、隶属于煤炭工业部的北京煤炭工业学校，1994年开始创办高等职业教育，1999年正式改制为职业技术学院。

Located in Shijingshan District, Beijing, Beijing Polytechnic College is a general higher vocational college organized by Beijing Municipal Government. It is one of the first batch of independent higher vocational colleges in China, a national model higher vocational college, and a presidium unit of the National Association of Presidents of Higher Vocational Colleges. It was formerly known as Beijing Coal Industry School, which was founded in 1956 and affiliated to the Ministry of Coal Industry. It began to establish higher vocational education in 1994 and was formally restructured as a vocational and technical college in 1999.

成就 Achievements

　　学校为北京市"特色高水平职业院校"建设单位以及中国特色高水平高职学校建设单位，先后获得全国高校就业工作50强、全国教学管理50强、全国教学资源50强、亚太职业院校影响力50强等。学校在全国职业院校教师教学能力大赛和学生技能大赛"双赛"中的成绩享誉全国。学校主要办学指标和综合办学实力位于国内同类院校前列，是全国最具影响力的高职院校之一。

Beijing Polytechnic College is the construction unit of High-Level Vocational Colleges with Special Characteristics in Beijing and the construction unit of High-Level Vocational Colleges with Special Characteristics in China. It has been awarded as one of the top 50 colleges in China in terms of employment, top 50 colleges in terms of teaching management, top 50 colleges in terms of teaching resources, and top 50 colleges in terms of influence in Asia Pacific vocational institutions. Its performance in the "Double Competition" of the National Vocational College Teaching Ability Competition and the Student Skills Competition is renowned nationwide. The main educational indicators and comprehensive educational strength of the college are among the forefront of similar institutions in China, and it is one of the most influential vocational colleges in China.

专业 Major

专科专业：
机电一体化技术、建筑工程、计算机网络技术、动漫设计与制作、移动互联应用技术、工商管理、旅游管理、会计等。

Specialized Majors:
Mechatronics Technology, Construction Engineering, Computer Network Technology, Animation Design and Production, Mobile Internet Application Technology, Business Management, Tourism Management, Accounting.

建校时间 Founding time	1956年	专业 Majors	27个专科专业
教师人数 Number of teachers	516	开学时间 Commencement time	秋季9月
学生人数 Number of students	约6000	学习年限 Years of study	3年制

报名联络 Registration Contact

通信地址：北京市石景山区石门路368号匠心楼305室
邮编：100042
联系电话：86-010-61801267
联系人：孟晴
电子邮箱：guohechu@bgy.edu.cn
学校网址：https://www.bgy.edu.cn

Address: Room 305, Jiangxin Building, No. 368 Shimen Road, Shijingshan District, Beijing, China
Postcode: 100042
Tel: 86-010-61801267
Contact: Meng Qing
Email: guohechu@bgy.edu.cn
Website: https://www.bgy.edu.cn

职教名校申请手册

学校介绍 School Profile

西安翻译学院
Xi'an Fanyi University

历史 History

西安翻译学院是由中国当代杰出教育家、民办教育拓荒者丁祖诒先生于1987年创办，座落在西安市南郊风景秀丽的终南山北麓、太乙河畔。学校2009年获得学士学位授予权；2013年顺利通过教育部本科教学工作合格评估；翻译专业获批2019年度首批国家级一流本科专业建设点，成为陕西 第一所获批国家级一流本科专业建设点的民办高校；2020年在软科中国大学排名中位居陕西民办大学第一；2021年新增2个国家级一流本科专业建设点，以拥有3个国家级一流专业建设点成为陕西省获得国家级一流专业建设点最多的民办高校，在全国民办高校中也以绝对优势遥遥领先，成为民办高校"双一流"建设的领跑者。经过30多年的办学实践，西安翻译学院已发展成为一所以文科、商科为主，以外语为特色，多学科协调发展，具有重要影响和鲜明特色的民办大学。

Xi'an Fanyi University was founded in 1987 by Mr. DING Zuyi, a prominent contemporary educator and pioneer of private education in China. It is located at the scenic north foot of Zhongnan Mountains and by the Taiyi River in the southern suburbs of Xi'an City. The university obtained the bachelor's degree-granting authority in 2009 and passed the Ministry of Education's undergraduate teaching qualification assessment in 2013. The major of Translation was approved as one of the first batch of national first-class undergraduate major construction sites in 2019, becoming the first private university in Shaanxi province to be approved as a national first-class undergraduate major construction site. In 2020, it ranked first among private colleges and universities in Shaanxi in Best Chinese Universities Ranking released by Shanghai Ranking. In 2021, the university added two more national first-class undergraduate major construction sites, and with three national first-class major construction sites, it becomes the only private university in Shaanxi with the largest number of national first-class major construction sites. And it also leads by a wide margin among private colleges and universities nationwide in the construction of "First-Rate Universities and Disciplines". After more than 30 years of schooling practice, Xi'an Fanyi University has developed into a private university with significant influence and distinctive features, with a focus on humanities and business, a characteristic of foreign languages, and coordinated development of multiple disciplines.

成就 Achievements

西安翻译学院始终坚持立德树人根本任务，学校先后被评为陕西省"平安校园"，陕西省教育系统"文明校园"；学校还获得"最具综合实力民办高校"和"最具就业质量奖"等荣誉称号。中央及省市权威媒体相继对学校的办学情况进行报道。

Xi'an Fanyi University has always adhered to the fundamental task of cultivating morality and educating people, and has been awarded the titles of "Safe Campus" in Shaanxi Province and "Civilized Campus" in the education system of Shaanxi Province. It has also been awarded "Private University with Most Comprehensive Strength" and "Private University with Highest Employment Rate". The central and provincial media have reported on its operation one after another.

专业 Major

学校下设英文学院、亚欧语言文化学院、教育学院、商学院、文学与传媒学院、艺术学院、工程技术学院、高级翻译学院、健康与运动学院、马克思主义学院、创新创业学院及继续教育学院共12个二级学院，以及体育部和公共艺术教育中心。学校开设本科专业36个、专科专业24个，涵盖文、经、管、工、艺、法、教育、医学等八大学科门类。

The university has 12 secondary colleges, including College of English, College of Asian and European Languages and Cultures, College of Education, College of Business, College of Literature and Media, College of Arts, College of Engineering and Technology, College of Advanced Translation, College of Health and Sports, College of Marxism, College of Innovation and Entrepreneurship, and College of Continuing Education, as well as the Department of Physical Education and the Center for Public Art Education. The university offers 36 undergraduate majors and 24 specialized majors, covering eight disciplines, including literature, economics, management, engineering, arts, law, education and medicine.

建校时间 Founding time	1987年	专业 Majors	本科专业36个，专科专业24个
教师人数 Number of teachers	1730余	开学时间 Commencement time	秋季9月、春季3月
学生人数 Number of students	25 614	学习年限 Years of study	1学期至4年不等

报名联络 Registration Contact

通信地址：陕西省西安市长安区太乙宫
邮编：710105
联系电话：86-029-85891138

Address: Taiyi Palace, Chang'an District, Xi'an City, Shaanxi, China
Postode: 710105
Tel: 86-029-85891138

职教名校申请手册

学校介绍 School Profile

陕西国防工业职业技术学院
Shaanxi Institute of Technology

历史 History

陕西国防工业职业技术学院于1958年建校，是一所由陕西省人民政府创办的全日制普通高等学校，2001年升格为全日制普通高等职业院校。建校以来，学院立足陕西，为中国科技工业和经济社会发展培养了大量创新型高素质技术技能人才。

Shaanxi Institute of Technology was found in 1958 as a full-time general higher education college by Shaanxi Provincial Government. In 2001, it was upgraded to a full-time general higher vocational college. Since its establishment, based in Shaanxi, the college has cultivated a large number of innovative and highly qualified technical and skilled talents for the development of China's scientific and technological industry and economic society.

成就 Achievements

全国职业教育先进单位、国家"双高"院校建设单位、国家示范性骨干高职院校建设优秀单位、国家优质高职院校、全国现代学徒制试点院校、教育部人才培养工作水平评估优秀单位、黄炎培职业教育奖优秀学校、陕西省"一流学院"立项建设单位、陕西省文明单位、陕西省职业教育先进单位、全国人工智能职业教育产教协同创新联盟执行理事长单位。

A national exemplary organization of Vocational Education, a construction unit of national "Double High-Level Plan" institutions, an outstanding construction unit of national model backbone higher vocational colleges, one of the national high-quality higher vocational institutions, one of the national modern apprenticeship pilot institutions, an excellent unit of talent training assessment of the Ministry of Education, one of the excellent colleges that won Huang Yanpei Vocational Education Award, a construction unit of Shaanxi Provincial "First-Class College" Project, a "Civilized Unit" of Shaanxi Province, an exemplary organization of Vocational Education in Shaanxi Province, and the Executive Director of National Collaborative Innovation Alliance of Vocational Education on Artificial Intelligence.

专业 Major

留学生招生专业：

数控技术、工业机器人技术、应用化工技术、电子信息工程技术、应用电子技术、计算机网络技术、软件技术、数字媒体技术、大数据技术、环境艺术设计、智慧健康养老服务与管理、机电一体化技术、道路与桥梁工程技术。

Majors for international students:

Numerical Control Technology, Industrial Robot Technology, Applied Chemical Technology, Electronic Information Engineering Technology, Applied Electronic Technology, Computer Network Technology, Software Technology, Digital Media Technology, Big Data Technology, Environmental Art Design, Smart Elderly Care Services and management, Mechatronics Technology, Road and Bridge Engineering Technology.

建校时间 Founding time	1958年	专业 Majors	58个
教师人数 Number of teachers	1000	开学时间 Commencement time	秋季9月、春季3月
学生人数 Number of students	18 000	学习年限 Years of study	1个月至3年不等

报名联络 Registration Contact

通信地址：陕西省西安市鄠邑区人民路8号
邮编：710300
联系电话：86-029-81480168
联系人：乔万俊；辛太隆
电子邮箱：Joangfxy@163.com
学校网址：https://www.gfxy.com

Address: No. 8, Renmin Road, Xi'an, Shaanxi, China
Postcode: 710300
Tel: 86-029-81480168
Contact: Qiao Wanjun; Xin Tailong
Email: Joangfxy@163.com
Website: https://www.gfxy.com

职教名校申请手册

学校介绍 School Profile

重庆工商大学派斯学院
Pass College of Chongqing Technology & Business University

历史 History

重庆工商大学派斯学院创办于1999年，2003年12月经教育部确认为全日制本科独立学院，是一所具有学士学位授予权的财经类普通本科高等学校。

Pass College of Chongqing Technology & Business University was founded in 1999 and approved as a full-time undergraduate independent college by the Ministry of Education in December 2003. It is a general undergraduate college of finance and economics with the right to confer bachelor's degrees.

成就 Achievements

学校的办学成就得到了政府和社会的高度评价和肯定，先后获得"重庆市学校社会力量办学先进单位""重庆市安全文明校园""全国最具品牌影响力独立学院""重庆市平安校园""全国民办教育先进单位"等荣誉。

The achievements of Pass College of Chongqing Technology and Business University have been highly acclaimed and affirmed by the government and society, and it has successively won the honors of "Exemplary Organization for Running Schools by Social Forces in Chongqing", "Safe and Civilized Campus in Chongqing", "Independent College with the Most Brand Influence in China", "Safe Campus in Chongqing", and "National Exemplary Organization of Private Education", etc.

专业 Major

本科专业：

会计学、工商管理、金融学、税收学、金融工程、保险学、信用管理、大数据管理与应用、市场营销、财务管理、审计学、物流工程、旅游管理、汉语言文学、英语、商务英语、新闻学、广告学、网络与新媒体、汽车服务工程、计算机科学与技术、物联网工程、数据科学与大数据技术、互联网金融、商务经济学、经济学、软件工程、跨境电子商务共28个专业。

There are 28 undergraduate majors including:
Accounting, Business Administration, Finance, Taxation, Financial Engineering, Insurance, Credit Management, Big Data Management and Application, Marketing, Financial Management, Auditing, Logistics Engineering, Tourism Management, Chinese Language and Literature, English, Business English, Journalism, Advertising, Network and New Media, Automobile Service Engineering, Computer Science and Technology, Internet of Things Engineering, Data Science and Big Data Technology, Internet Finance, Business Economics, Economics, Software Engineering, and Cross Border E-Commerce.

建校时间 Founding time	1999年	专业 Majors	28个本科专业
教师人数 Number of teachers	900余	开学时间 Commencement time	秋季9月
学生人数 Number of students	13 000余	学习年限 Years of study	4年

报名联络 Registration Contact

通信地址：重庆市合川区交通街593号

邮编：401520

联系电话：86-023-42889197

联系人：陈流星；杨国馨

电子邮箱：paisizjc@126.com

学校网址：https://www.paisi.edu.cn

Address: No. 593, Jiaotong Street, Hechuan District, Chongqing, China
Postcode: 401520
Tel: 86-023-42889197
Contact: Chen Liuxing ; Yang Guoxin
Email: paisizjc@126.com
Website: https://www.paisi.edu.cn

职教名校申请手册

学校介绍 School Profile

重庆人文科技学院
Chongqing College of Humanities, Science & Technology

历史 History

重庆人文科技学院的前身是2000年创办的西南师范大学行知育才学院，几经更名，2013年经教育部批准转设为由重庆市教委主管的普通本科高校。学校是全国应用技术型大学战略试点研究高校、重庆市硕士专业学位研究生教育培育试点单位。

The predecessor of Chongqing College of Humanities, Science & Technology is Xingzhi Yucai College of Southwest Normal University founded in 2000, and its name had been changed for several times. In 2013, it was approved by the Ministry of Education to transform into a general undergraduate university under the supervision of Chongqing Municipal Education Commission. It is one of the national strategic pilot research institutions among applied technology oriented institutions in China, and a pilot unit for cultivating postgraduates with Professional Master's Degree in Chongqing.

成就 Achievements

学校荣获"全国民族团结进步创建示范单位""全国先进社会组织""中国民办高等教育优

秀院校""中国民办教育百强""全国生态文明教育特色学校""全国红十字模范单位""重庆市第二届教育综合改革试点成果三等奖""重庆市民族团结进步模范集体""重庆市绿色学校建设示范学校"等荣誉称号。

Chongqing College of Humanities, Science & Technology has won multiple honorary titles, such as "National Exemplary Organization for Ethnic Unity and Progress", "National Advanced Social Organization", "Excellent Institutions of Private Higher Education in China", "Top 100 Private Education in China", "National Ecological Civilization Education Featured Schools", "National Red Cross Model Organization", "Third Prize of the Second Chongqing Comprehensive Education Reform Pilot Achievements", "Chongqing Model Group for Ethnic Unity and Progress", "Chongqing Model School of Green School Construction".

专业 Major

汉语言文学（师范）、汉语国际教育（师范）、新闻学、法学、思想政治教育（师范）、经济学、金融工程、工程管理、会计学、英语（师范）、人力资源管理、物流管理、供应链管理、旅游管理、酒店管理、学前教育（师范）、机械设计制造及其自动化、机械电子工程、车辆工程、汽车服务工程、新能源科学与工程、电子信息工程、数学与应用数学（师范）、计算机科学与技术、软件工程、信息安全、物联网工程、数据科学与大数据技术、通信工程、护理学、建筑学、风景园林、园林、设计学类（视觉传达设计、环境设计、服装与服饰设计）、美术学（师范）、音乐表演、音乐学（师范）、舞蹈学、表演、广播电视编导、播音与主持艺术、社会体育指导与管理等46个专业。

There are 46 majors such as Chinese Language and Literature (Teacher), Chinese International Education (Teacher), Journalism, Law, Ideological and Political Education (Teacher), Economics, Financial Engineering, Engineering Management, Accounting, English (Teacher), Human Resource Management, Logistics Management, Supply Chain Management, Tourism Management, Hotel Management, Preschool Education (Teacher), Mechanical Design, Manufacturing and Automation, Mechanical Electronic Engineering, Vehicle Engineering, Automotive Service Engineering, New Energy Science and Engineering, Electronic Information Engineering, Mathematics and Applied Mathematics (Teacher), Computer Science and Technology, Software Engineering, Information Security, Internet of Things Engineering, Data Science and Big Data Technology, Telecommunications Engineering, Nursing, Architecture, Landscape Architecture, Gardening, Design Category: Visual Communication Design, Environmental Design, Costume and Clothing Design, Fine Arts (Teacher), Music Performance, Musicology (Teacher), Dancology, Performance, Radio and Television Editing, Broadcasting and Hosting Art, Social Sports Guidance and Management.

建校时间 Founding time	2000年	专业 Majors	46个本科专业
教师人数 Number of teachers	近1800	开学时间 Commencement time	秋季9月
学生人数 Number of students	近23 000	学习年限 Years of study	4年或5年

报名联络　Registration Contact

通信地址：重庆市合川区草街街道学院街256号重庆人文科技学院

联系电话：86-023-42465352；42464905；42465342

联系人：蒋明

学校网址：https://www.cqrk.edu.cn

邮编：401524

电子邮箱：zsc@cqrk.edu.cn

Address: No. 256, College Street, Caojie Street, Hechuan District, Chongqing, China

Tel: 86-023-42465352；42464905；42465342

Contact: Jiang Ming

Website: https://www.cqrk.edu.cn

Postcode: 401524

Email: zsc@cqrk.edu.cn

学校介绍 School Profile

湖北职业技术学院
Hubei Polytechnic Institute

历史 History

  湖北职业技术学院是1998年经原国家教育委员会批准，由原孝感教育学院和原国家级重点中专孝感市卫生学校、孝感市财贸学校、孝感市机电工程学校合并组建的一所全日制综合性普通高职院校(命名为孝感职业技术学院)，地处湖北省孝感市。2003年，经湖北省人民政府批准，孝感职业技术学院更名为湖北职业技术学院。经过多年的发展，湖北职业技术学院已融入地方经济社会发展，成为办学条件完善、办学水平高、职教特色鲜明、综合性、高水平高职院校。

Hubei Polytechnic Institute is a full-time comprehensive general vocational college. Its predecessor was Xiaogan Vocational and Technical College, incorporated by the former Xiaogan Education College, the former national key technical secondary school Xiaogan Nursing school, Xiaogan Finance and Trade School, and Xiaogan Mechanical and Electrical Engineering School in 1998, approved by the former National Education Commission. It is located in Xiaogan City, Hubei Province. In 2003, with the approval of Hubei Provincial Government, Xiaogan Vocational and Technical College was renamed as Hubei Polytechnic Institute. After years of development, Hubei Polytechnic Institute has been integrated into the local economic and social development, becoming a comprehensive and high-level higher vocational college with complete schooling conditions, high educational level, distinct vocational education characteristics.

成就 Achievements

2008年获评国家高技能人才培养示范基地，2010年获评国家示范性高职院校，2014年获评第四届黄炎培职业教育奖"优秀学校"，2019年获评国家优质专科高等职业院校，2019年入选国家"双高计划"建设单位；2021年牵头成立的湖北护理职业教育集团入选教育部示范性职业教育集团培育单位；多次获评湖北省职业教育先进单位、湖北省大学生创业示范基地、湖北省服务区域经济发展先进高校、湖北省普通高等学校毕业生就业工作先进集体、湖北省文明单位等荣誉称号。

In 2008, Hubei Polytechnic Institute was awarded the National High-Skilled Talents Training Model Base. In 2010, it was awarded the National Model Higher Vocational College. In 2014, it was awarded the Excellent School of the Fourth Huang Yanpei Vocational Education Award. In 2019, it was awarded the National High-Quality Specialized Vocational Institute. In 2019, it was selected as the construction unit of the national "Double High-Level Plan". In 2021, the Hubei Nursing Vocational Education Group, whose establishment was proposed initially by Hubei Polytechnic Institute, was selected as a model vocational education group training unit by the Ministry of Education. It has won many honorary titles, such as Hubei Exemplary Organization of Vocational Education, Hubei Model Base of Entrepreneurship for College Students, Hubei Advanced Institute for Serving Regional Economy, Advanced Group for Graduate Employment in Hubei colleges and universities in Hubei Province, and Hubei Civilized Unit.

专业 Major

专科专业：

护理、软件技术、临床医学、口腔医学、建筑技术、数控技术、汽车检测与实验技术、学前教育、酒店管理与数字化运营、电子信息工程技术等。

Specialized Majors:

Nursing, Software Technology, Clinical Medicine, Stomatology, Building Technology, Automotive Testing and Laboratory Technology, Preschool Education, Electronics, Hotel Management and Digital Operation, Electronic Information Engineering Technology, etc.

建校时间 Founding time	1951年（中职）1998年（高职）	专业 Majors	44个专科
教师人数 Number of teachers	995	开学时间 Commencement time	秋季9月、春季3月
学生人数 Number of students	18 000	学习年限 Years of study	1学期至3年不等

报名联络 Registration Contact

通信地址：湖北省孝感市玉泉路17号
邮编：432000
联系电话：86-0712-2868612
联系人：丁争柱
电子邮箱：936469311@qq.com
学校网址：https://www.hbvtc.edu.cn

Address: No. 17, Yuquan Road, Xiaogan City, Hubei, China
Postcode: 432000
Tel: 86-0712-2868612
Contact: Ding Zhengzhu
Email: 936469311@qq.com
Website: https://www.hbvtc.edu.cn

学校介绍 School Profile

重庆城市管理职业学院
Chongqing City Management College

院校风采 Institutional Charm　　**任波** REN Bo

重庆城市管理职业学院任波教授
REN Bo, Professor of Chongqing City Management College

任波

　　管理学博士，二级教授，国务院政府特殊津贴获得者、重庆市有突出贡献的中青年专家、首届重庆市高校中青年骨干教师，兼任重庆市高等教育学会第四届理事会副会长、中国高等教育学会第七届理事会理事，在《中国高等教育（CSSCI核心版）》等核心期刊发表论文10余篇，主编《社会管理创新研究》《社会福利机构经营与管理》《社会福利机构活动策划与组织》，主持教育部国际合作与交流司、民政部、重庆市社会科学规划重大项目等国家级、省部级及以上课题10余项。作为第一完成人，先后获国家级教学成果二等奖1次、重庆市教学成果一等奖1次。

Doctor of Management, Second-Tier Professor, is the recipient of the Special Government Allowance of the State Council, a Young and Middle-Aged Expert with Outstanding Contribution in Chongqing, one of the first batch of young and middle-aged backbone teachers in Chongqing colleges and universities, the vice president of the fourth council of Chongqing Higher Education Association and the director of the seventh council of Chinese Higher Education Association. He has published more than 10 papers in core journals such as *Chinese Higher Education (CSSCI Core Edition)*, compiled several books such as *Research on Social Management Innovation*, *Social Welfare Institution Operation and Management*, and *Social Welfare Institution Activity Planning and Organization*, and presided over more than 10 national, provincial and ministerial level and above research topics under the Department of International Cooperation and Exchange of the Ministry of Education, the Ministry of Civil Affairs and the Chongqing Social Science Planning Major Projects. As the first author, he has been awarded the second prize of national teaching achievement once and the first prize of Chongqing teaching achievement once.

历史 History

重庆城市管理职业学院始建于1984年，是由重庆市人民政府举办、中国民政部与重庆市人民政府签约共建的公办全日制普通高等学校，位于重庆高新区大学城。学校是全国文明校园、中国特色高水平专业群(A档)建设单位、国家优质院校、国家骨干院校。

Chongqing City Management College, founded in 1984 by Chongqing Municipal Government, is a full-time public higher education institution, sponsored jointly by the Ministry of Civil Affairs of China and Chongqing Municipal Government. It is located in the University City of Chongqing High-Tech Zone. It is a national civilized campus, a construction unit of high-level major cluster with Chinese characteristics (A grade), a national high-quality institution, and a national backbone institution.

成就 Achievements

学校积极服务"一带一路"建设，坚持扩大对外开放，稳步推进国际化办学战略，形成了"五维一体"的国际化办学模式，曾连续3年获得中国高职院校"国际影响力50强"荣誉，是重庆市高校国际交流先进单位。2021年学校"中文+职业技能"国际推广平台建设项目获得重庆市国际化特色项目立项，2022年学校成功入选中国教育国际交流协会第五批"中国—东盟高职院校特色合作项目"，并成为"中国—东盟职业教育联合会"发起单位、教育部国际司"中德先进职业教育合作项目首批试点院校"。

The college actively serves the construction of the "Belt and Road", insists on expanding the opening to the outside world, steadily promotes the strategy of international education, and has formed a "five-dimensional integrated" internationalization mode. It has won the honor of "Top 50 International Influence" of Chinese higher vocational institutions for three consecutive years, and is the exemplary organization of international exchanges among colleges and universities in Chongqing. In 2021, the construction project of "Chinese + Vocational Skills" international promotion platform was approved as an international characteristic project in Chongqing. In 2022, it was selected as one of the fifth batch of "China-ASEAN Vocational Institutions Specialized Cooperation Project" by China Education Association for International Exchange, and became the initiator of "China-ASEAN Vocational Education Federation" and one of the first batch of pilot institutions of the "Sino-German Advanced Vocational Education Cooperation Project" by the International Department of the Ministry of Education.

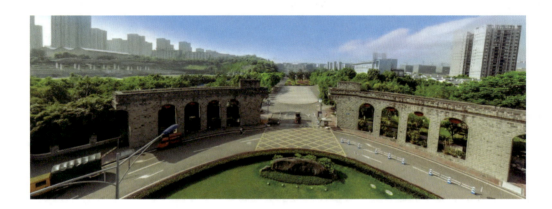

专业 Major

留学生招生重点专业：
会计、现代物流管理、园林工程技术、康复工程技术 、护理、跨境电子商务、国际经济与贸易、社会工作。

Key majors for international students:
Accounting, Modern Logistics Management, Landscape Engineering Technology, Rehabilitation Engineering Technology, Nursing, Cross-Border E-Commerce, International Economics and Trade, Social Work.

建校时间 Founding time	1984年	专业 Majors	45个
教师人数 Number of teachers	989	开学时间 Commencement time	秋季9月、春季3月
学生人数 Number of students	17 322	学习年限 Years of study	6个月短期非学历留学生或者 3年全日制学历留学生

报名联络 Registration Contact

通信地址：重庆市高新区虎溪大学城南二路151号

邮编：401331

联系电话：86-023-65626161(党政办)；023-65626666(招生处)；
　　　　　023-65626066(国际合作与交流中心)

电子邮箱：419156902@qq.com

Address: No. 151, South 2nd Road, Huxi University City, High-tech Zone, Chongqing, China
Postcode: 401331
Tel: 86-023-65626161 (College Party and Administrative Office); 023-65626666 (Admissions Office);
　　　023-65626066 (International Cooperation and Exchange Center)
Email: 419156902@qq.com

职教名校申请手册

学校介绍 School Profile

重庆应用技术职业学院
Chongqing Vocational College of Applied Technology

历史 History

重庆应用技术职业学院前身是陶行知先生于1946年创办的社会大学，2005年经重庆市人民政府批准、教育部审定备案，设立为重庆市教育委员会主管的全日制普通高等学校。学院位于重庆合川区大学园区，紧邻多所高等院校，具有浓郁的文化氛围和丰富的教育资源支撑。学院文体设施齐全，学习生活环境优雅，是重庆市平安校园。

Chongqing Vocational College of Applied Technology, formerly a social university founded by Mr. Tao Xingzhi in 1946, is a full-time general higher education institution approved by Chongqing Municipal Government and validated for the record by the Ministry of Education in 2005, under the supervision of Chongqing Municipal Education Commission. The college is located in the University Park of Hechuan District, Chongqing, close to many colleges and universities, with a vibrant cultural atmosphere and rich educational resources. The college has complete cultural and sports facilities and an pleasing learning and living environment, making it a safe campus in Chongqing.

成就 Achievements

近年来，学院人才培养质量稳步提升。新专业评估及骨干专业建设均通过验收；"1+X"技能等级证书工作和职业培训工作深入推进，各级各类研究课题和项目数量逐年攀升。学院师生在省部级及以上各类教学竞赛、职业技能竞赛、文体比赛及创新创业比赛中屡获佳绩。近两年，教师获得省级以上教学比赛奖10余人次、获得省级骨干青年教师专项荣誉称号10余人次；学生多次荣获"巴渝工匠"杯重庆市高等职业院校学生职业技能竞赛、"外研社·国才杯"英语比赛、全国高职院校学生汽车营销技能大赛及"国艺杯"艺术设计比赛一、二、三等奖；文体项目在大学生文艺展演、啦啦操、街舞、田径、跆拳道、网球、拳击等项目中均斩获佳绩。

In recent years, the quality of talent cultivation in the college has steadily improved. Both the evaluation of new majors and the construction of backbone majors have passed the acceptance; The "1+X" project of skill level certificate and vocational training have been deeply promoted, and the number of research topics and projects at all levels has been increasing year by year. The faculty and students of the college have repeatedly achieved excellent results in various teaching competitions, vocational skills competitions, cultural and sports competitions, and innovation and entrepreneurship competitions at the provincial and ministerial levels. In the past two years, the teachers have won more than 10 provincial-level or above teaching competition awards and more than 10 provincial-level backbone young teacher special honorary titles; the students have won multiple awards in the Chongqing "Bayu Craftsman Cup" Vocational Skill Contest, the "FLTRP National Talent Cup" English Competition, the National Vocational College Student Automobile Marketing Skills Competition, and the "National Art Cup" Art Design Competition, and also achieved good results in all sorts of cultural and sports activities, such as the College Students Art Show, the Cheerleading Competition, the Street Dance Competition, Track and Feld Events, Taekwondo Competition, Tennis Games, and Boxing Match.

专业 Major

专科专业：

学前教育、早期教育、艺术教育、健康管理、智慧健康养老服务与管理、社区康复、婴幼儿托育服务与管理、药品经营与管理、旅游管理、酒店管理与数字化运营、社会体育、计算机网络技术、大数据技术、软件技术、信息安全应用技术、数字媒体技术、移动互联应用技术、电子商务、网络营销与直播电商、智能物流技术、大数据与会计、大数据与财务管理、汽车制造与试验技术、新能源汽车技术、汽车电子技术、汽车智能技术、工程造价、建设工程监理、建筑工程技术、智能建造技术、建筑设计共31个专业。

There are 31 undergraduate majors including:
Preschool Education, Early Education, Art Education, Health Management, Smart Elderly Care Service and Management, Community Rehabilitation, Infant and Child Care Service and Management, Drug Business and Management, Tourism Management, Hotel Manage

ment and Digital Operation, Social Sports, Computer Network Technology, Big Data Technology, Software Technology, Information Security Application Technology, Digital Media Technology, Mobile Internet Application Technology, E-Commerce, Online Marketing and Live Streaming E-Commerce, Intelligent Logistics Technology, Big Data and Accounting, Big Data and Financial Management, Automobile Manufacturing and Testing Technology, New Energy Automobile Technology, Automobile Electronics Technology, Automobile Intelligent Technology, Engineering Cost, Construction Project Supervision, Construction Engineering Technology, Intelligent Construction Technology, and Architectural Design.

建校时间 Founding time	2005年	专业 Majors	31个本科专业
教师人数 Number of teachers	400余	开学时间 Commencement time	秋季9月
学生人数 Number of students	8000余	学习年限 Years of study	3年

报名联络 Registration Contact

通信地址：重庆市合川区思源路60号

邮编：401520

联系电话：86-023-42463556

学校网址：https://www.cqyyzy.com

Address: No.60, Siyuan Road, Hechuan District, Chongqing, China
Postcode: 401520
Tel: 86-023-42463556
Website: https://www.cqyyzy.com

学校介绍 School Profile

云南大学滇池学院
Dianchi College of Yunnan University

历史 History

云南大学滇池学院是由云南省唯一的"双一流"大学云南大学申办并经教育部批准的独立学院。作为云南省规模最大的独立学院,自2001年创办以来,凭借云南大学先进的办学理念、雄厚的综合实力和学校灵活的办学机制,已经形成经、法、教育、文、理、工、管、艺术多学科协调发展,以培养高素质应用型创新人才为主的普通本科高等学校。

Dianchi College of Yunnan University is an independent college organized by Yunnan University, the only "Double First-class" university in Yunnan Province, and approved by the Ministry of Education. As the largest independent college in Yunnan Province, since its establishment in 2001, Yunnan University has formed an ordinary undergraduate college with coordinated development of economics, law, education, arts, science, engineering, management and art, focusing on cultivating high-quality applied and innovative talents, relying on its advanced educational concepts, strong comprehensive strength, and flexible educational mechanisms.

成就 Achievements

学校是唯一获得国家教育部"全国高校毕业生就业工作50强""全国高校毕业生创新创业工作50强""全国深化创新创业教育改革示范高校""全国高校毕业生就业能力培训基地""国家级创新创业教育实践基地"荣誉的独立学院。学校是唯一获得3届中国"互联网+"大学生创新创业大赛全国金奖的独立学院。

Dianchi College is the only independent college that has been awarded the "Top 50 National Graduates Employment Work", "Top 50 National Graduates Innovation and Entrepreneurship Work", "National Demonstration Universities for Deepening Innovation and Entrepreneurship Education Reform", "National Graduates Employment Ability Training Base" "National Innovation and Entrepreneurship Education Practice Base" by the Ministry of Education. Dianchi College is also the only independent college that has won the national gold medal of the 3rd "Internet+" College Students Innovation and Entrepreneurship Competition in China.

专业 Major

本科专业：

经济学、金融学、国际经济与贸易、工商管理、市场营销、人力资源管理、物流管理、行政管理、法学、社会工作、社会体育指导与管理、休闲体育、汉语言文学、汉语国际教育、新闻传播学类（新闻学、广播电视学、广告学）、英语、日语、泰语、商务英语、数学与应用数学、电子信息工程、通信工程、人工智能、计算机科学与技术、软件工程、信息安全、物联网工程、数字媒体技术、数据科学与大数据技术、土木工程、工程管理、工程造价、建筑学、城乡规划、会计学、财务管理、数字经济、创业管理、电子商务、音乐表演、舞蹈学、播音与主持艺术、动画、绘画、视觉传达设计、环境设计、产品设计、服装与服饰设计、数字媒体艺术、艺术与科技等52个本科专业。

There are 52 undergraduate majors including:
Economics, Finance, International Economy and Trade, Business Administration, Marketing, Human Resources Management, Logistics Management, Administration, Law, Social Work, Social Sports Guidance and Management, Leisure Sports, Chinese Language and Literature, Chinese International Education, Journalism Communication Studies (Journalism, radio and television, advertising), English, Japanese, Thai, Business English, Mathematics and Applied Mathematics, Electronic Information Engineering, Telecommunications Engineering, Artificial Intelligence, Computer Science and Technology, Software Engineering, Information Security, Internet of Things Engineering, Digital Media Technology, Data Science and Big Data Technology, Civil Engineering, Project Management, Project Cost, Architecture, Urban and Rural Planning, Accounting, Financial Management, Digital Economy, Entrepreneurship Management, E-commerce, Music Performance, Ddance, Broadcasting and Hosting Art, Animation, Painting, Visual Communication in Environmental Design, Product Design, Clothing and Fashion Design, Digital Media Art, Art and Technology, etc.

建校时间 Founding time	2001年	专业 Majors	52个本科专业
教师人数 Number of teachers	近1461	开学时间 Commencement time	秋季9月
学生人数 Number of students	25 000余	学习年限 Years of study	4年或5年

报名联络 Registration Contact

通信地址：云南省昆明滇池国家旅游度假区红塔东路2号
邮编：650228
联系电话：86-0871-64316805；64313233
联系人：蔡煜
学校网址：https://www.ynudcc.cn

Address: No. 2 Hongta East Road, Dianchi National Tourism Resort, Kunming City, Yunnan, China
Postcode: 650228
Tel: 86-0871-64316805；64313233
Contact: Cai Yu
Website：https://www.ynudcc.cn

2024

1
January

SUN 周日	MON 周一	TUE 周二	WED 周三	THU 周四	FRI 周五	SAT 周六
	1	2	3	4	5	6
7	8	9	10	11	12	13
14	15	16	17	18	19	20
21	22	23	24	25	26	27
28	29	30	31			

本月纪要
Monthly Summary

2024

2
February

SUN 周日	MON 周一	TUE 周二	WED 周三	THU 周四	FRI 周五	SAT 周六
				1	2	3
4	5	6	7	8	9	10
11	12	13	14	15	16	17
18	19	20	21	22	23	24
25	26	27	28	29		

本月纪要
Monthly Summary

2024

3
March

SUN 周日	MON 周一	TUE 周二	WED 周三	THU 周四	FRI 周五	SAT 周六
					1	2
3	4	5	6	7	8	9
10	11	12	13	14	15	16
17	18	19	20	21	22	23
24	25	26	27	28	29	30
31						

本月纪要
Monthly Summary

2024

April

SUN 周日	MON 周一	TUE 周二	WED 周三	THU 周四	FRI 周五	SAT 周六
	1	2	3	4	5	6
7	8	9	10	11	12	13
14	15	16	17	18	19	20
21	22	23	24	25	26	27
28	29	30				

本月纪要
Monthly Summary

2024

5
May

SUN 周日	MON 周一	TUE 周二	WED 周三	THU 周四	FRI 周五	SAT 周六
			1	2	3	4
5	6	7	8	9	10	11
12	13	14	15	16	17	18
19	20	21	22	23	24	25
26	27	28	29	30	31	

本月纪要
Monthly Summary

2024

6
June

SUN 周日	MON 周一	TUE 周二	WED 周三	THU 周四	FRI 周五	SAT 周六
						1
2	3	4	5	6	7	8
9	10	11	12	13	14	15
16	17	18	19	20	21	22
23	24	25	26	27	28	29
30						

本月纪要
Monthly Summary

2024

7
July

SUN 周日	MON 周一	TUE 周二	WED 周三	THU 周四	FRI 周五	SAT 周六
	1	2	3	4	5	6
7	8	9	10	11	12	13
14	15	16	17	18	19	20
21	22	23	24	25	26	27
28	29	30	31			

本月纪要
Monthly Summary

2024

8
August

SUN 周日	MON 周一	TUE 周二	WED 周三	THU 周四	FRI 周五	SAT 周六
				1	2	3
4	5	6	7	8	9	10
11	12	13	14	15	16	17
18	19	20	21	22	23	24
25	26	27	28	29	30	31

本月纪要
Monthly Summary

2024

9
September

SUN 周日	MON 周一	TUE 周二	WED 周三	THU 周四	FRI 周五	SAT 周六
1	2	3	4	5	6	7
8	9	10	11	12	13	14
15	16	17	18	19	20	21
22	23	24	25	26	27	28
29	30					

本月纪要
Monthly Summary

2024

10
October

SUN 周日	MON 周一	TUE 周二	WED 周三	THU 周四	FRI 周五	SAT 周六
		1	2	3	4	5
6	7	8	9	10	11	12
13	14	15	16	17	18	19
20	21	22	23	24	25	26
27	28	29	30	31		

本月纪要
Monthly Summary

2024

11
November

SUN 周日	MON 周一	TUE 周二	WED 周三	THU 周四	FRI 周五	SAT 周六
					1	2
3	4	5	6	7	8	9
10	11	12	13	14	15	16
17	18	19	20	21	22	23
24	25	26	27	28	29	30

本月纪要
Monthly Summary

2024

12
December

SUN 周日	MON 周一	TUE 周二	WED 周三	THU 周四	FRI 周五	SAT 周六
1	2	3	4	5	6	7
8	9	10	11	12	13	14
15	16	17	18	19	20	21
22	23	24	25	26	27	28
29	30	31				

本月纪要
Monthly Summary